THE *Girl* INSIDE

A Handbook for Beautiful Living

Mary Burkholder

The Girl Inside

Mary Burkholder
92 Z. C. Rushing Road
Tylertown MS 39667
mary@maryburkholder.com

ISBN: 978-1-7334328-1-8

Cover and interior design: Sheila Bauman
Cover photo: Shutterstock

All scripture quotations are from the King James Version unless otherwise noted.

All definitions provided by Oxford Languages, part of Oxford University Press.

Printed by Carlisle Printing
Printed in the United States of America

For my daughters, Hannah and Lila—

may you grow ever more beautiful on the inside

Contents

Chapter One

Body Image

We live in a world obsessed with what we can see and largely unconcerned with what we can't see. That means people think more about their bodies than their souls. Our culture emphasizes women's physical beauty so much that every woman alive probably feels that she doesn't measure up in some area. Beauty seems complicated and confusing. We may worry God did not make us beautiful enough.

Many women try to hide their inner emptiness and corruption and focus on enhancing and preserving their visible attributes. They believe the lie that their appearance is the most important thing about them. That message is not from God. God made our bodies. "God saw everything that he had made, and, behold, it was very good" (Genesis 1:31). Our bodies are good. They are imperfect. They are all different, but God made them the way he wanted them.

You can be confident in who you are in Christ. As a Christian, your security is not based on your appearance. You can have the eternal beauty of a soul at peace with God—the inner beauty of the "hidden man" (1 Peter 3:4). The Greek words have the idea of the "secret person." This secret, eternal part of us is where true beauty and worth reside, no matter what society may say.

A BIT OF HISTORY

Women have always wanted to look pretty. However, before the 1900s, as a general rule girls were more concerned with their characters and less concerned with appearance. If you have read the old classics, you know what I'm talking about. Girls lamented their rudeness, un-lady-likeness, or lack of charity and resolved to improve their characters—think of Jo March in *Little Women*. In the introduction to *The Body Project: An Intimate History of American Girls*, Joan Jacobs Brumberg writes that diaries from the 1800s mention girls' struggles to improve their behavior and be better people. They were not as obsessed with their bodies' imperfections.[1]

In the 1900s, girls' diaries became full of worries about their bodies. They obsessed over their acne, weight, and lack of physical development. Today, many women are highly preoccupied with their physical appearance and very little with their character. My mother always said, "Pretty is as pretty does." And mothers have a way of being right about things.

Too often in today's culture, people value women's bodies almost more than anything else about them. One of the primary reasons for this focus is the influence of media and the entertainment world. Celebrities generally have beautiful faces and perfect bodies. Their looks seem to matter more than their actual talents at times. These celebrities are admired and emulated by many in a way that can only be described as worship.

Likely you don't personally spend a lot of time following celebrities, but we all feel some social pressure to have nice bodies. Our culture faithfully reminds us to think about our bodies at every opportunity. Think of the many places that allure women to spend money on their bodies: hair salons, gyms and fitness centers, tanning salons, and nail salons. We see these all the time, even if we do not frequent them.

We drive by billboards offering magical surgical solutions for losing weight or altering body parts we don't like. In the store checkout line, the beautiful models on magazine covers accuse us of being below average. In newspapers and magazines, online and by junk mail, we are bombarded with ads for weight loss, fad diets, health foods, and supplements.

Consumerism has seized upon the body insecurity promoted by the media, making us spend money on our outward appearance. Consider the amount of shopping space dedicated to personal care items in a department store. When you finally locate the thing you want, you must decide which kind of it you want out of ten, fifteen, or more options. Reading the labels only makes you think about your body in more detail. *Do I want whitening, fluoride-free, or sensitive toothpaste? Should I buy the generic brand or the expensive healthful stuff? Do I need shampoo for kinky, straight, fine, or greasy hair? Which product has the best scent?* Instead of locating what we need and moving on, we can spend quite a bit of time over decisions in the personal care section. Surrounded by all this, it's impossible not to think about our bodies!

MODELING CRITERIA

The rigid beauty standards of the modeling industry can

cause women's normal concerns about their appearance to become obsessive. The media constantly places the few bodies which meet their criteria in front of the whole country. This tends to make the average woman feel like she is one of only a few women who doesn't have the correct look, when she is actually among the majority. The models are in the minority—in other words, only models look like models.

And standards in today's modeling industry are becoming increasingly unrealistic. Not only must models have well-proportioned faces, but their body proportions must also meet strict criteria. The average model weighs twenty-three percent less than the average woman.[2] While increasing obesity may exaggerate this percentage, the disparity cannot be ignored. The current media ideal of thinness can be achieved naturally by very few women, and if you add the requirement of a beautiful face and the right height, the look is even rarer. You are not alone if you don't look like a Hollywood star or even the women in clothing catalogs.

Unsurprisingly, models have a hard time living up to the expectations of their appearances: they keep strict diets which frequently lead to eating disorders. They typically fast or dehydrate themselves before photo shoots.[3] Additionally, their photos are usually still airbrushed to accent the curves of their bodies.[4] Models aren't having all that much fun; it seems absurd that other women should yearn to be like them.[5]

Our culture seems to tell us that there is one basic beauty standard. But God does not have only one beauty standard; this is obvious in the diverse way he designs us. For example, the ideal model must be tall, but more than a few women worldwide are shorter than the ideal. If God thought tall was the most beautiful, he could have easily made all women taller. Instead, we come in all heights. He designs us with different skin tones, hair colors, hair types, eye colors, facial symmetry, and body shapes. God obviously finds beauty in diversity, and our diversity shows His creativity. It is a lie that we should all strive and pine after a single look. The devil always wants to twist the truth and make us believe the opposite.

Culture tells us we are never pretty enough. The Bible tells us we are precious and beautiful in God's eyes:

- We are fearfully and wonderfully made (Psalm 139:14). God himself designed us with attention to detail.
- We are created in the image of God (Genesis 1:27). I am not prepared to expound on the theological possibilities of this statement, but to be compared in any way to the divine is an incredible concept.
- We are daughters of God (2 Corinthians 6:18). What could give us greater security than a divine father?
- Our bodies are temples of the Holy Spirit (1 Corinthians 6:19, 20). Imagine: divinity dwells in our physical bodies.
- Our bodies are living sacrifices (Romans 12: 1, 2). God intends for us to use our bodies to serve him; they have far greater value than mere outward appearance.

AVERAGE AND HAPPY

It is also a lie that we must have a specific look to be attractive to men. In general, women are beautiful for simply being female. It is true that men can be affected by cultural dictates of female beauty, but on the whole, a pleasant woman who takes an average amount of care with her appearance is attractive. Men are obviously attracted to different types of women because all kinds of women get married, not just tall ones with symmetrical facial features.

We can get so hung up on our outward appearance that we forget the importance of being nice. Our culture is so loud about appearance that we may get the impression that this is all men care about; this is far from true. Personality and behavior matter. Any man would like to be married to someone beautiful in soul: a kind, happy, comfortable person they will enjoy growing old with. No man wishes to marry a beautiful but temperamental woman. A happy woman tends to be remembered as more beautiful than she is because of her pleasant expression and manner. There are many average-looking—or what our culture would consider below-average-looking—women enjoying life and married to men who consider themselves fortunate. We all like to be around someone who is likeable and makes us feel accepted.

A sweet face and kind character will do more for a woman's appearance than any makeup or surgery. Our faces and eyes show our feelings and reflect our souls; in the end, they are our most important features. A smile is an effective and simple facelift. This kind of attraction comes from within, from the girl inside.

LET'S TALK ABOUT YOUR BODY

Which of these statements best describes your opinion of your body?

- I'm mostly okay with it—wouldn't change much.
- I like it—wouldn't change anything.
- I don't like most of my features—wish I could exchange my body for another.

I encourage you to think seriously about which body-image

option best describes you. Unless you've been hiding under your bed for the last ten or fifteen years, you are not entirely unaware of what our culture considers beautiful. Likely it affects you on some level. It would be healthy to consider how much it affects you and whether you believe cultural lies or God's truths about your body.

Random comments from our childhood and youth can shape our concept of what constitutes beauty and affect how we view our bodies. For example, if someone comments positively on our thinness, we may feel secure in that. Consequently, we may feel we have lost an essential part of our identity if we gain weight.

If you have ever received a positive compliment on some aspect of your appearance, likely you feel satisfied with that part of yourself. But if someone made fun of your features, you may hate the part of you they criticized. This can cause you to believe something about yourself that is merely the unkind opinion of one or two people. The painful truth is—it's possible that person didn't even mean it. Maybe they were just trying to be funny or impress someone by being mean. Maybe they were jealous of you in some way.

If you were slightly more than skinny as a child and someone called you fat—or you imagined someone insinuated you were fat—you may internalize this as a bitter truth and struggle with feeling overweight, even if you're not.

Are there things like this in your past that shaped the way you think about yourself? It may have been a too-outspoken grandmother or aunt, the girl who was jealous of you, the perverted teasing boys. Words can be so carelessly spoken and forgotten by one, so remembered and believed by another. If you struggle with body image, take a few minutes to consider what has shaped the way you feel about yourself. You may be telling yourself something that is not true. It can be liberating to identify such moments from the past and realize: *This is why I am so obsessed with this. It was just someone's words. It does not need to define me.*

Don't make negative comments about your body, not even to yourself. When you look in the mirror, your eyes tend to go straight to the part of your body you're dissatisfied with. Maybe you're tempted to criticize the feature you don't like, hoping someone will quickly reassure you that it's not as bad as you think. Instead, take it to God and tell him about it. God's assurance will mean far more to you.

God does not look at our bodies and see what is wrong with us. He created us. It cannot make him happy to see us standing before a mirror thinking or saying what we don't like about ourselves. A simple idea for deciding whether we believe truth or lies about ourselves is to put "God my father says..." before the statement. "God my father says my hips are too big." That's terrible, isn't it?

If you identify with the option of really hating your body, seek God's truths about bodies and immerse yourself in them. Get your Bible and a concordance and search for verses about the creation of man and woman and God's care for humanity. Maybe start a new journal and use it to make notes of things you identify with as you read this book. Use these thoughts as a starting point for personal study and reflection as you seek to grow more lovely in soul. Never forget that the incorruptible (KJV) or "imperishable" (ESV) beauty of the girl inside is very precious in God's sight (1 Peter 3:4). Your physical body will reach a peak and begin to deteriorate. Your inward loveliness can grow forever, untarnished and unfading.

Chapter Two

Thin Culture

One of the most common body image problems in the western world is a concern about being thin enough. Women have long wished to be slender. They cinched themselves into torso-shaping corsets from the sixteenth century to the twentieth. Remember Laura's Aunt Docia and Aunt Ruby in *Little House in the Big Woods* tightening each other's corset strings before a dance, gasping "pull harder!" as they squeezed the breath out of each other? We may smile at the silly vanity that made them suffer in tight corsets all evening simply to achieve the coveted hourglass figure. But modern women are no less silly. Twenty-first-century women endure a lot in their attempts to slenderize.

Over the years, women shed the layers of clothing they once wore, and the corset went out of fashion. You can't very well wear a corset with a two-piece bathing suit, skinny pants, or a midriff-exposing shirt. You need to be truly thin, not just squeezed in. Therefore, it's no surprise that women in the 1970s and 1980s turned to diet, exercise, and even surgery in their attempts to achieve the small-waisted look.

The fashion industry is mainly responsible for this. Fashion designers want super-tall, very thin women (and men) to model their clothing. The irony of modeling is that it all masquerades as beauty. But stories by models tell another side. Models are often treated poorly. They are sometimes demeaned into losing incredible amounts of weight. The competition is so stiff that they frequently develop eating disorders.[1]

Why so thin? One reason seems to be that fashion modeling is about the clothes. The models are human hangers. Designers want them to be long-legged and gaunt to emphasize the beauty of the clothes.[2]

An anorexic model may continue to suffer physically and allow herself to be mistreated because her body has become her worth. Hearing her agent praise her skeletal look and getting a chance to walk the runway is worth that much to her. This obsession shows the absurdity of getting our worth from our bodies.

The whole world does not share this preoccupation with slenderness. Some cultures find extra pounds on a woman attractive: it shows her status—she is well-off financially because she obviously has enough to eat. One reason our culture looks down on extra weight is because this is reversed. Wealthy people in America can afford to eat healthier. There seems to be a subconscious, lower-class association with cheap carbs: chips, prepared foods, McDonald's takeout, and the subsequent weight gain. We are quick to associate weight with class, even though, as Christians, we are taught to avoid partiality and class distinction.

Christians need to be honest with these cultural influences. What sector of our society should we identify with? Where are we getting our cues? Criticizing and belittling heavier people, being obsessed with our weight, or praising others for their slim figures is an unhealthy place to be.

DIETING

No one is born with a compulsion to lose weight. Generally, babies make their desire to eat known very clearly. We worry if they don't seem to have an appetite. Mothers are pleased with small children who like to eat and anxiously coax their picky eaters. Somewhere, in some way, the idea of restricting our food intake and consequently our size may be introduced to our minds. Think about your journey: is this a struggle for you? What has influenced the way you think about dieting?

We are bombarded with options for diets, weight loss plans, and toning workouts. Most women are concerned with their weight to some extent. Even if they do nothing about it, the feeling that they should lurks in the back of their minds.

The primary definition of *diet* is simply "the food you usually eat." For example, the diet of a cow is grass. Diet has come to mean "a particular course of food restricting one's intake to become healthier or lose weight." As a verb, the word means "limiting food intake to lose weight." Because of our cultural obsession with thinness, this last definition is usually the first to come to mind when we think of the word.

Specific diets make waves from time to time, such as the keto, Mediterranean, paleo, and South Beach diets. These are called *fad diets*. A fad diet is a popular diet that is scientifically unproven. It involves restriction in some way, often by removing certain types of food, such as carbohydrates. The diet may initially help someone lose weight, but is not usually sustainable. Fad diets can cause health problems if our bodies are deprived of essential nutrition for a long period of time. Be wary of such diets. Remember: if something sounds too good to be true, it probably is.

If you truly are overweight, dieting is still not a good solution. You may lose weight on a diet only to regain it when you stop dieting. It is better to make permanent lifestyle changes, such as establishing portion control, eliminating or reducing sugar, exercising regularly, and eating more vegetables. A diet will only work long-term if it can be used permanently. If you have been a heavier person all your life, losing weight may be challenging and nearly impossible. Part of our appearance is due to genetics. Whether we like our body size or not, we all need to choose to accept how we look.

I distinctly remember the first time I heard about dieting. A person with an influential personality, who was no more overweight than I was, commented that she was trying to lose weight. I instantly thought I should lose weight too. I was a sturdy fourteen-year-old farm girl. I could heave square bales, hoist fifty-pound bags of feed, and tote two five-gallon buckets full of water, and I had an appetite to match. Thankfully my weight loss program was short-lived; I couldn't deal with the hunger.

EATING DISORDERS

There are those with more self-restraint than I had, those who believe false messages about their body size to the point of restricting their nourishment so much that they damage their health. This problem is known as an eating disorder. Two common eating disorders are anorexia and bulimia. Anorexia is "an emotional disorder characterized by an obsessive desire to lose weight by refusing to eat"; bulimia, "an emotional disorder involving distortion of body image and an obsessive desire to lose weight, in which bouts of uncontrolled eating are followed by depression and self-induced vomiting, purging, or fasting."

With the constant cultural pressure to be thin, it is no coincidence that eating disorders are on the rise. Studies have shown that twenty percent of college-aged women are anorexic or bulimic. Up to forty percent of college-aged women sometimes display some of these behaviors.

If your struggle with dieting goes to these extremes, you must seek help. Clues that your struggle is severe enough to need help include trying to deceive others about the amount of food you are eating, becoming obsessive about having an eating ritual—eating certain things in specific amounts at definite times—or no longer having your monthly period.[3] If this describes you, start by talking to one trusted person.

One complication that can fuel eating disorders is the weight gain many girls experience during puberty. Part of this is caused by the development of the curves of womanhood; sometimes, it is due to an increase in appetite as the body stores extra fat to prepare for impending growth spurts. If girls are already paying attention to their weight and body shape, they may panic and try to diet. Unfortunately, this is the worst thing they could do. Their developing bodies and newly activated hormones need nourishment. Depriving the body of necessary nutrition can stop a woman's monthly cycle, wreck her hormones, and be detrimental to her health for years, even the rest of her life.

An eating disorder is not a body problem but a mental problem; we believe something untrue about ourselves. A girl who feels insecure may think that controlling her weight will be a solution. She may soothe her anxiety with a rigid eating routine and food intake. Being in control of her body may make her feel she has control in all areas of her life. Of course, it is only an illusion of control; in reality, it is bondage. She will never be thin enough when she looks in the mirror.

All women should realize that having a distorted body image is common. It's difficult to prove, but it has been said that every woman sees herself as larger than she is when she looks in the mirror. As a young woman, I was naturally thin and never dieted—not after that first brief attempt—but now, looking at pictures of myself then, I know that I never viewed myself as being as thin as I really was.

IS THINNER HAPPIER?

Weight loss ads, fitness programs, pictures of models, and billboard advertisements convey an unspoken message that being thin equals being happy. Unknowingly, we can internalize the concept that losing weight would make us feel happier. All those skinny models you see in advertisements are flashing big smiles or seductive stares: their bodies have power, which equals happiness, according to our culture.

The cult of thinness has become a sort of religion in America. Naturally, women who aren't spiritually fulfilled are most attracted to it. Is the decline of religion in America connected with body obsession? Are women seeking spiritual security in this physical manifestation? If this is the case, Christian women should not need to join this search for personal security. We know where our security is: God made our bodies. They belong to him. We want to use our bodies to serve him.

As Christians, we know in our heads that being thin won't truly bring us security and happiness. Yet we live in these so-visible bodies in this so-thin culture. How do we deal with the effects of the cultural worship of thinness?

Maybe you are overweight, and you eat for comfort when anxious or depressed. Losing the weight is not the solution; you need to address the sadness. Bingeing is a different kind of disordered eating. If you struggle with uncontrollable cravings and find yourself gorging on chocolate cake at midnight, don't hate yourself for your lack of control. Instead, think about what drives that craving. Pray. Journal your feelings. Cry. Search for scripture verses about God's comfort. God cares about you and your sadness. He is the "God of all comfort" (2 Corinthians 1:3). It's also important to find someone you trust with whom you can share. God speaks to us and encourages us through other Christians.

An important part of receiving God's comfort is sharing it with others. God comforts us so that we are "able to comfort them which are in any trouble" (2 Corinthians 1:4). Getting our minds off ourselves by helping others can lift our mood. It is also good to remember that feeling sad is not necessarily bad. We live in a fallen, imperfect world. We are sinful people who make bad choices that we regret sometimes. Jesus said: "Blessed are they that mourn: for they shall be comforted" (Matthew 5:4).

IS THINNER HEALTHIER?

Being thin has become synonymous with being healthy, but I suspect this is a bit of a cloak to make the thin agenda less conspicuous. We all feel that losing weight is more righteous if we're doing it to become healthier. As Christians, we know we should take care of our bodies, so if being unhealthy is wrong, being anything other than thin must be wrong. We need to be careful with this.

It is true that the average American diet is less than the healthiest; we have a lot of not-so-good-for-us options on the grocery shelves. We also have unlimited access to food and can easily be unbalanced in our consumption. This imbalance is one reason diets specific to improving health have gained so much traction. If we want to use a particular diet, we must remember that God designed our bodies to need nutrients from all the basic food groups. We can upset our bodies' complex and fragile systems by denying them the nutrition they need.

It's foolish to assume that thinner people are healthy and heavier people are unhealthy. Remember, God designed our bodies in different shapes and sizes. An overweight person might have an underlying health problem, but so might an underweight person. Culturally we tend to be far more critical of the heavier person than the thin one. We should remember that weight is not an automatic barometer of physical or spiritual health.

A BALANCED VIEW

We don't want to be in bondage to eating disorders or to compulsively try diet after diet. We want to be free of the diet-culture mindset, healthy and happy with our bodies in their God-intended size. We need to analyze our motives and be honest with the desires of our hearts.

If you are obsessed with losing weight, try to analyze why. Are you insecure, imagining that being noticed and praised for weight loss will raise your self-esteem? Are you lonely, secretly hoping that being thinner will attract attention? Are you jealous of someone prettier, thinner, and more popular? Losing weight will not solve these problems. Consider the state of your relationship with God: are you doing your best to live in obedience to him? We must ask ourselves hard questions and bring the real answers before God. We can have profound insecurities about our body image that cause pain and turmoil, but the solution may not be what we think it is.

When you have figured out the bottom-line reason that you want to lose weight, see if it lines up with what God wants for you. If you desire attention, you need to learn how to appropriately fill the desires of your heart—getting thinner is not a spiritual solution. If you feel unhealthy, you should focus on what your body needs, not primarily on weight loss. Becoming healthier *may* help you lose weight, but losing weight will not automatically make you healthier. Find out what your body needs and pay attention to what your diet does for you. If you are on a special diet and feel terrible, your body is not coping well. No weight loss is worth potential health problems.

If you are consumed with thoughts and plans for how to eat less and exercise more, you probably need to step away from your obsession with your weight loss and refocus. Find someone to share with who can help you develop a healthy body image.

Don't get caught up in celebrity news and tabloid gossip: we don't need to know the names of famous artists and actresses, who is paired with whom, or who is winning the awards. The entertainment world is so much about bodies, exposure, and immoral behavior; allowing ourselves to be sidetracked in this way will negatively affect us. We become like those we admire. Deliberately choose real, down-to-earth, everyday Christian role models: women who handle life with grace, are content to be themselves, and whose inward loveliness shines through imperfect bodies.

God calls us to much loftier goals of loveliness than what the world offers us. It must grieve his heart when insecurities and self-loathing consume us. These bodies are vessels God gave us to do good and to serve him, to become his hands and feet to those around us.

The world may judge by what they see on the outside, but God sees directly into our hearts (1 Samuel 16:7). And even though culture blasts us with a different message, the girl inside is far more important than outward appearance.

Chapter Three

Modesty Defined

Is modesty about the outside or the inside of us? Modesty has *something* to do with our outward appearance, but it has *everything* to do with the inside. It is not entirely about clothes, but it is partly about clothes. As something we put on, clothes reveal something about the girl inside.

Modesty for women has been so emphasized and belabored in conservative circles that I almost hate to bring it up. I believe it has, at times, been taught with incorrect associations that have fueled resentment and confusion; however, modesty is a biblical principle. We will look at it once more, hopefully without muddying the waters further.

The dictionary definition that applies to the kind of modesty we're talking about has to do with appropriate or decent appearance and behavior. We all recognize indecency when we see it, but we can get stuck on where the line is for decency.

MODESTY FROM THE BIBLE

Basic modesty is instinctual: we read in Genesis that when Adam and Eve understood their nakedness, they hid from God. They tried to dress themselves before God helped them get dressed (Genesis 3:9-11). God did not need to sit down with them and explain why they should wear clothes. The awareness of their sinfulness and of God's holiness caused them to recognize the nakedness of their bodies and souls. Unless people have been hardened to accept exposure of their bodies, everyone naturally puts on at least a few clothes. Our culture has somehow decided that all that is required is that the most private parts be covered. This bare minimum modesty may go to ridiculous extremes in tight and skimpy clothing that misses the point of dressing.

Modesty is closely tied to our feelings of self-worth and our security in Christ. Our security in a close relationship with Christ and other Christians will help prevent us from immodest behavior and dress. We may be tempted sometimes to feel that modesty hampers our popularity and hides our beauty. Proverbs 31:30 reminds us that popularity and beauty are worthless, and our actual value rests in proper awe and reverence for God. Again, it's not about the outside but the inside of you.

When conservative Christians talk about modesty, the emphasis tends to be placed on women's clothing and usually involves particular applications. Modesty does involve women's clothing, but I will not be super-practical here. I'm not going to tell you how long your sleeves ought to be or how to wear your sweaters. I presume I am talking to young women who have had plenty of teaching on this, young women who already dress very modestly by the world's standards. Your church and your parents tell you what is expected of you regarding clothing specifics. I would like to talk about some broader aspects.

One aspect of modesty we don't always think about is our behavior; this involves behaving appropriately and maturely and not drawing unnecessary attention to ourselves. We will talk more about appropriate behavior in the next chapter.

CLOTHING

We need to talk about clothing because it makes up a large portion of the appearance we present to the world. Our clothes send messages. According to one fashion model, our clothes send a message about our values and beliefs whether or not we care about it or take control of the message. [1]

What are you saying with your clothes?

- I want to submit to God's direction and my church and parents.
- I don't think it's important to submit to anyone; it doesn't matter what I wear.
- I need to wear this to be in style, to fit into the right group of young people.

If we struggle with what we are asked to wear and desire things we are asked not to wear, we need to look inside our hearts and see what motives drive our clothing choices. You may think that the problem is that your church group or your parents are unnecessarily restrictive, but you should ask yourself why you desire more liberty. Why are certain items or colors of clothing so important to you? Why would you want to wear clingy fabric or use a more revealing pattern? You will find much more spiritual freedom in submitting to "unnecessary" rules than in restlessly chafing under them.

I speak as one who once thought I could never be part of a

church that dressed more conservatively than the one where I was raised, but who ended up doing exactly that. It did not kill me to dress more conservatively. In fact, it has benefitted me. It had little to do with the clothes themselves, but laying down my will in this area did benefit me spiritually.

Besides what is going on in our own hearts, we can't escape the fact that our clothes influence those around us. Our clothes may influence younger or weaker women to make better or worse choices. Our clothes may create unrest and distrust among our peers if we push the boundaries of what is acceptable in our setting. What kind of influence do you want to be? Why would you want to be the trendsetter, always on the edge of the latest fad? Why not model the accepted standard? If you are an influential person, you should take your influence seriously.

Maybe you are not a popular, influential person. You want to wear what the popular girls are wearing so you can be accepted by them. You want to wear a jacket with the "right" logo to the youth function. You'd like to sit beside them on Sunday morning and casually stick your cute and trendy shoes out to be noticed. Your primary motive may not be a desire to be immodest or extravagant, but the clothing you crave to wear so you can be accepted is outside your parent's boundaries for you. It is not easy to feel left out of your peer group simply because of what you wear, but you will never regret cheerfully submitting to your parents.

If you find yourself the goody-goody in your youth group, look at it as an opportunity to grow in beauty on the inside. It is your opportunity to be so nice and friendly that others can't help but like having you around, no matter what you wear. Take the challenge to set an example rather than be a follower. You will find true security in submitting to Christ and your parents, not in being part of the cool group.

Women like clothing. Little girls love a new dress, and so do big girls. We like variety and originality. We want to look nice. This combination can lead to tension with our churches and our parents on what is appropriate and what is not. Obviously, there is not one prescribed dress standard that is perfect. We can see variations in what is acceptable among conservative groups. You may look at what other presumably godly women are doing and feel resentment: "I don't need to dress like this to be saved." "God knows my heart." "The Bible doesn't tell us to dress like this."

We are missing the point if we focus on these arguments. We all have a natural inclination to push toward the outer edges of what is acceptable, but this is a carnal response, the human heart's attraction to the forbidden. The Bible teaches that church leaders will be held responsible for the spiritual well-being of their members. "Obey them that have the rule over you and submit yourselves: for they watch for your souls, as they that must give account, that they may do it with joy and not with grief" (Hebrews 13:17). It also teaches that children should obey their parents. "Children, obey your parents in the Lord; for this is right" (Ephesians 6:1).

Clothing guidelines must become practical at some point. A pastor can preach eloquently on principles of modesty only to find his message interpreted differently by different listeners. Somewhere between a burka and a bikini bathing suit, there is a line. Your church and parents take on the responsibility of saying where they will place that line. Honoring that line is the safest and healthiest place for you to be.

You could argue that you desire to follow Christ, and therefore he will guide you in your clothing choices, but the more serious we are about following Christ, the more we welcome input from other Christians. An independent Christianity where no one but God has the right to speak to me is not scriptural. God himself established the concept of church and fellowship of believers. We reject God and his plan for Christians if we say we do not need anyone else. Struggling to accept directives from your authorities indicates a lack of trust and submission. Choose to believe that they have your best interests in mind rather than doubting them and assuming the worst. Your attitude will make all the difference. The style of dress pattern or the brand of shoes is not the most important thing; your soul, the girl inside, is the most important.

The biblical definition of modesty indicates that our clothing should not draw undue attention to ourselves and that our beauty should not come from outward adornment (1 Peter 3:3; 1 Timothy 2:9). *Adorn* means "to decorate or add unnecessary touches." Adorning could include bold colors, exotic prints, or innovative designs, something that is different from what everyone else is wearing. Why do we want to draw attention to ourselves? The goal of a Christian should be to draw attention to Christ, not ourselves.

Biblical concepts of immodesty also include extravagance, expensive clothing, and a too-large wardrobe. There is more to life than being the best-dressed woman with the latest fabrics and patterns. Why would we spend extra for the name on the jacket or shoes? Is it truly a higher quality choice, or are you paying more simply for the brand? How many dresses are practical and responsible? Ten? Fifty? How many sweaters and jackets do you need to go with them? One woman explained that she keeps a certain number of hangers in her closet; she does not buy another dress until she takes an old one out of her closet. Having a limit is not a bad idea. Sweaters and jackets in neutral colors can be mixed and matched with various dresses, rather than brighter colors that may only match one dress.

If we can afford to buy expensive clothing and a lot of clothing, maybe we should consider giving more money away. It is also a good idea to save money. There may come a day when you have a family and need to budget more closely. You will find it difficult if you are in the habit of being extravagant.

Jesus calls us to a life of simplicity, focused on service. It is not hard for us to admire Jesus as a simple person wearing simple, homespun garb. But it is another thing to be like him.

IS MODESTY BECAUSE OF MEN?

Modesty has become a loaded topic partly because of an emphasis on being modest for the sake of men and their visual temptations. This concept was pushed strongly by the evangelical purity movement of the 1990s. The idea was that if girls would dress better, boys could behave better. There is an element of truth in this, but it creates problems when taught as the primary reason for women's modest dress. It can come across as something like this: women's bodies are so beautiful that they cause men all kinds of lust problems; we need to cover up and hide our bodies from their animalistic and uncontrollable reactions.

I recall the confusion and resentment I felt when I was first exposed to this teaching. Why did I have to take on this massive responsibility of controlling male lust? I feared the power of my own body—a power I could presumably wield unknowingly. I felt anxious because I wanted to like and trust the men I knew. I felt confused because men are supposed to be spiritual leaders; how could I ever respect a husband who could not control himself?

And then there is the question: what does a man do when confronted with the immodesty and immorality permeating our culture? If a man needs a woman to dress modestly to keep him from sinning, he is apparently expected to fail when faced with immodesty.

Biblical modesty is something appropriate to do *for ourselves.* It is something appropriate to do around women as well as men, and particularly before God. Christian men indeed appreciate being around modest women. But they are fully responsible for their own thoughts and actions. Men will answer to God for wrong thoughts. Women will answer to God for dressing inappropriately.

Men can and do control themselves when in compromising situations. Think of Joseph when seduced by Potiphar's wife (Genesis 39:3-12). But they should not have to face such situations in their homes and churches. Men appreciate being able to relate comfortably with women who do not dress in a way that draws attention to parts of their bodies that should not be in focus. A Christian man doesn't want his thoughts to go to the wrong place any more than you do.

It is true that men have visual temptations on a level that women generally do not. An unmarried woman likely cannot fully understand this. This is not your worry. Being in obedience to your church and your parents keeps you in a safe place so that you can be appropriate without understanding all the reasons why. If your mother attempts to teach you to be ladylike, be grateful. Much of what we call "ladylike" is just modest, appropriate behavior, much more than something out of the archives of an old-fashioned finishing school. Such teaching includes sitting up straight rather than lounging, keeping your knees close together, moderating your voice, and using caution when sitting in low places and rising from them.

We dare not flip to the opposite extreme and say it doesn't matter what we wear because men are responsible for themselves; this is a common reaction to the purity culture movement. This concept seems to flip all the responsibility for purity back onto the men, rather than sharing it.

Some teach that women should be able to dress just as they please because there is no difference between men and women. We know that there *are* differences. The Bible tells us that men and women have distinct roles. Nature itself provides evidence of differences between us. God created us with these differences and called them good. We respect God's design and accept our place in it when we embrace modesty.

CONSERVATIVE APPEARANCE

Ironically enough, as a woman who wears attire that is ultra-conservative by the world's standards, you probably attract nearly as many glances as an immodest woman—though for a different reason. Cultural dictates would encourage us to feel inferior about our appearance because it contradicts everything they say women's clothing should be. They uncover and flaunt. We cover and conceal. But I encourage you not to sneak apologetically about town, trying not to meet anyone's eyes. Own your look—not in a haughty or self-righteous way, but as one who is happy and comfortable being herself. You have every right to be at home and natural in your conservative garb. An older gentleman I met in town once blessed me by saying the way I dressed was "so beautiful." I generally assume I look odd to people, not beautiful.

Don't be afraid of stares and questions. I remember how

hard it can be as a shy teenager to explain why you look like you've dropped in from another era or just had a part in a play. I recall a youth trip outing when a young woman curiously asked a group of us girls, "Why y'all wear dem hats?" referring to our head coverings. I slipped away, leaving the more outspoken ones to explain. Many years later, I realized she had not said *dumb* hats. She had been merely curious, not mocking.

Even if you fully believe in what you do, it can be hard to explain when you're nervous and put on the spot. Don't stress over it. A simple answer is usually satisfactory. You don't need to go into deep theological explanations. And don't try to parrot someone else. Just be yourself and answer simply. If the asker wants more details, offer the phone number of your dad or pastor. Whatever you choose to say, don't mumble that your parents or your church make you do this. Even if you've been born and raised in your church setting, it is your choice to embrace your culture. You are part of the church you are in. If you are a church member, you have agreed to its standards. Embrace your appearance as part of the choice you made for Christ.

Chapter Four

Becoming Behavior

Modesty also involves our behavior. The way you conduct yourself reveals quite a lot about the girl you are inside. A Christian woman should use behavior that "becometh" godliness (Titus 2:3). *Becometh* means befitting[1] or appropriate to the occasion. A godly woman's behavior matches up with the holiness and purity in her heart.

Too much chatter, silly behavior, and loud laughter can be a form of immodesty or indecency. Proverbs 11:22 says that a fair woman without discretion is like a jewel of gold in a pig's nose. In other words, beauty and uncontrolled behavior just don't go together. A beautiful, nicely dressed young woman who behaves indiscreetly is just as incongruous as something lovely and valuable in the pig pen. Her behavior does not match up with holiness.

I would like to focus primarily in this chapter on relating appropriately to young men. This topic can be tricky. Is it okay to talk to the boys? When is it alright to talk to the boys? What subjects are appropriate? Is it okay to have a special friend who is a boy but not a boyfriend? Unless you live in a nunnery, you likely struggle with questions like these. Depending on the backgrounds, personalities, and social expectations of particular locales and church affiliations, what is considered appropriate—or more likely inappropriate—can vary widely. For this reason, I cannot present a convenient one-size-fits-all solution.

If I say you should not have an extended conversation with a young man, some will find that hopelessly old-fashioned. If I say it is healthy for boys and girls to discuss ideas as a group, some will think it presents a disturbing breakdown of reserve. For this reason, I will avoid offering much practical application. However, there are basic principles to consider which will guide your behavior.

Before we start on how to behave, it would be good for you to consider your idea of a romantic relationship. You may think this is beside the point because you are not establishing a romantic relationship with all the young men in your life, just trying to figure out how to relate appropriately. But what you expect from romance will affect how you relate to all young men. You must clearly understand that true love is not about fulfilling your desires. We tend to be selfish when we think of romantic relationships: *What's in this for me?* Cultural concepts of romance encourage us in thinking this way. But romantic and sexual longings are not intended primarily for self-fulfillment.

Inside the boundaries God has established, these desires create a strong bond with one person and provide a secure foundation for a family unit. Romance is not all about what you can get out of it but how you can also bless your partner. For this reason, you need to control your desires for romance until it is the right time and way to express them. If both you and your potential future spouse control your desires until you meet each other, you will have a secure foundation for a committed marriage and a happy home.

When you focus on your desire for romantic fulfillment and are not willing to respect boundaries, you will find yourself tempted to grab for things that are not yours. You may stoop to snatching bits of romance wherever and however you can: seeking attention from young men, being available to a special relationship outside the proper boundaries of an official courtship, maybe even aggressively pursuing a young man's attention. This behavior is based on taking, not giving, and will lead to heartache and disappointment.

Giving instead of taking means considering others. Is your behavior defrauding young men, offering hints of romance but leaving them confused about your intentions? If your exchanges with young men could be captured as videos and played for their future wives, would you be pleased with how you'd behaved? Or if your future husband could watch how you related, would you be embarrassed? As a sister in Christ, how can you be a blessing to the young men in your life?

You may think that living with boundaries is outdated and keeps everyone from having fun. This is what our culture tells us. Our culture encourages young people to throw away every restraint and act like animals in a guiltless free-for-all. If you believe your body evolved at random, then your body has no purpose, and it doesn't matter what you do with it. But people are not animals. Their bodies did not evolve, and each body contains a living soul. We cannot turn off our souls. People who date freely and sleep with whoever they feel like at the moment will suffer. They may seem to be having a good time for a while, but their souls cry in the silence and bleed from the pain they inflict on themselves. The Bible teaches us the guidelines we need to be at peace with ourselves. No one can change the rules for happy living; they can only pretend to.

Obeying godly principles is very freeing and provides the security we crave. A chaste lifestyle focused on giving and serving and a pure courtship at the right time leads to a secure and faithful marriage. Self-restraint creates space for personal peace, mutual fulfillment, and secure family life. Don't be deceived. Our culture's careless attitudes toward romantic and sexual relationships are not bringing anyone happiness. The many broken hearts are evidenced by abuse, addictions, depression, murders, and suicides. People destroy their happiness when they toss away God's standards for life.

We may be tempted to think we can "sow wild oats" and live as we please for a while, then get our lives together and serve God later. We cannot do this without suffering the consequences. The Bible teaches that we will reap what we sow (Galatians 6:7). This means our actions will certainly have consequences. God forgives sin, but his forgiveness does not erase the effects we have to deal with. A few minutes of "harmless fun" can haunt you in subtle ways for the rest of your life.

APPROPRIATE BEHAVIOR

We find some basic guidelines for appropriate behavior for young women in Titus 2:4, 5:

- Sober: disciplined and sensible.[2]
- Discreet: self-controlled and moderate.[3]
- Chaste: clean and innocent.[4]

What might *sober* mean for women's behavior? It does not mean we can't laugh, joke, and enjoy ourselves. The biblical definition implies being in control of oneself, remaining calm and collected, not acting as though drunk. It is okay to have a good time, but not to become giddy to the point of silly intoxication so that you blush to remember it the next day. It can be surprisingly easy to become giddy when having a good time with an attractive young man. It might be helpful for you to consider recent interactions you've had with young men and think about whether you should blush at your behavior. I am not talking about falling into self-humiliation and being mortified by having made a silly mistake or not being as witty as you wanted to be. Some personality types can get too caught up in reliving every interaction and beating themselves up for their stupidity: if this is you, please stop right away! I'm not talking to you. Other personalities could benefit from more introspection. I am talking about saying foolish things, being too loud, and laughing too much.

Being *discreet* involves good judgment in appearance, both in dress and behavior. A synonym of discreet is *unobtrusive*. It can be fun to be the center of attention, but a godly woman does not seek to be in the limelight. She does not need to tell all the stories and get all the laughs. She is not afraid to be a "wallflower," because her security doesn't come from getting attention.

On the other hand, it is true that the chatty girls are the ones who keep the conversation flowing and make everyone feel comfortable. If your personality is more talkative, you can be a blessing in a group setting. A true conversationalist will guide the topic to deflect attention to others, attempting to draw everyone into the discussion. If it is easy for you to talk, make it your goal to get others talking about themselves, including the quieter ones in the group.

Being discreet also involves behaving wisely. One way to judge your discretion level is to ask yourself if you act differently in a mixed setting than when you are with girls only. This is a bit of a tricky question because we all tend to behave a little differently when relating to the opposite gender. This is normal. But if being around the boys gives you a rush that makes you act out of character, that is a red flag. Another test to consider for a mixed setting: can you still talk to girls, or do you focus primarily on talking with the boys in the group?

In some ways, there should be a marked difference in the way you relate to young men and to your girlfriends. It might be okay to nudge a girlfriend when sharing a joke, but there is no reason for a young woman to pat, shove, nudge, or otherwise be in physical contact with any man who is not her husband. Being discreet includes restraining yourself from impulsive and thoughtless behavior.

Discretion includes not saying everything that pops into your head. Maybe you have a lovely opportunity to make a joke at someone else's expense, to join in making fun of someone, or to share a juicy piece of gossip. Saying it would get everyone's attention; maybe they would consider you witty, and perhaps you'd feel "in" with the popular group. If it's not kind or wise, don't say it. If you wouldn't want your parents to overhear it, don't say it. Knowing when to speak and when not to speak is a mark of maturity. A strong urge to say something may indicate it would be better off left unsaid.

Chaste means free of impurity, particularly sexual impurity. Purity involves far more than keeping one's virginity. It involves private thoughts and actions. If we are not pure in our private lives, we will find it more difficult to know where the boundaries are in relating to others. We need an entire lifestyle of purity.

Pure living includes controlling our emotions. It is normal to notice handsome young men with pleasant personalities. It is normal for some of these young men to be at the top of your list of men you consider eligible for marriage. But this doesn't mean you should allow yourself to be consumed by crushes. Just as you control your body's behavior, you need to manage your thoughts and emotions. You may think you can keep your thoughts separate from your behavior, but our thoughts inform our actions; we act based on what we think. Sooner or later, unrestrained thoughts tend to sneak out in unrestrained behavior. We will talk more about emotional purity in the following chapter.

PRE-DATING

Let's talk about this quasi-relationship thing known as *pre-dating*. You're not officially dating a young man, but the two of you are unofficially an item. Your friends know you like each other. You're experimenting with attraction and putting some feelers toward each other to see if this might develop into something more. For a young man, it might be a way to test the waters and figure out how a girl feels about him before he goes to all the work of asking her and jumping through potential dad-in-law hoops.

Young people who are involved in pre-dating run into a lot of problems. Often the couple is too young to date formally. Maybe their parents want them to wait until they are eighteen, nineteen, or twenty-one to date, but their claims have been staked with each other since high school or even middle school. A clandestine, undefined relationship may feel like innocent excitement, but I have observed that such behavior often leads to insecurity and heartache. How can you know for sure what an undefined relationship means to the other person? It's kind of awkward to ask a young man if you're his girlfriend if he never officially asked you for a date. If one of you "falls out of love" or is convicted to end the relationship, how do you tell the other person it's over when it never formally began? Suppose you reach the age your parents will permit you to date, but he doesn't ask; you don't know what you mean to him or whether you should wait for him. You can hardly say, "Hey, my dad says I'm old enough to date now," if he's never made his intentions clear toward you. He may have never considered you girlfriend material at all. He may call you a good friend and have his eye on another girl. If you talk to friends about your feelings for him, it could get around to him and become awkward. You may think this kind of confusion would not happen to you, but when our feelings get involved, we tend to see things biased in the way we want to see them.

High school romances can drift into marriage without a young man ever formally asking a girl to date him. Such careless courting is not a secure way to begin a marriage. A relationship that has no clear beginning leaves much room for insecurity and doubt. Such relationships tend to begin in secrecy and deception, and the sneaky behavior may raise doubts about each other's fidelity later. *He snuck around to see me; would he do it again? He took advantage of me emotionally; can I trust him?* You may imagine this is not a big deal, but it could have long-term effects on your marriage. Why take chances?

Perhaps your parents will not allow you to date the young man you desire, so you hang out together behind their backs, perhaps aided and abetted by friends. It's not too hard to see that this is a dangerous place to be. You are headed for trouble if you disobey your parents and spend time with a young man of supposed questionable character without accountability. Disobedience sets the stage for immoral behavior. If your boyfriend sees that you are willing to step outside the boundaries of obedience, he may naturally suppose you are willing to go farther with him physically than you ever intended. When you get into a difficult spot in your relationship with him, you will have no one to turn to for support and guidance because you are going against the authorities in your life.

Pre-dating is emotionally consuming and will occupy large portions of your time, energy, and thoughts at a time in your life when you should be free to focus on other things. Your girlhood is a formative time when you have the opportunity to do many things, grow personally, and establish bonds with family and friends undistracted by romantic attachments. Enjoy this freedom; it is not something to chafe against.

GUIDELINES FOR RELATIONSHIPS

A good rule of thumb is to treat all the boys the same until one formally asks you. I know this can be hard if you have feelings toward someone. It may be easy to act yourself around a young man you do not consider eligible but difficult around someone who makes your heart beat faster. It is a good exercise in self-discipline to control your feelings and hide them from others. You cannot help being attracted to certain young men, but you can help what you do with those feelings. Don't allow yourself to be controlled by temptations to try to be where he is and get his attention. Don't drop hints that you like him through conversation or mutual friends. You will feel most secure in a relationship where the young man made the first move.

This is not to say you should be cold and rude. Your warm

and impartial friendship should extend to all young men equally, whether you see them as suitable for boyfriends or not. Instead of picturing each one as a potential husband, try to imagine each as likely being someone else's husband someday.

Don't make yourself too readily available to a special relationship. If a young man hints that he'd like to get to know you better, make clear what it will take for that to happen. If he gives you special attention and tries to engage you in intimate conversation, make it clear you are not available in that way. If he talks to you about beginning a relationship and your dad has made it a prerequisite that a suitor ask him first, tell him that. This is not about playing hard to get, but about keeping feelings within appropriate boundaries and establishing clear guidelines for relationships. Marriage is a serious life-long commitment and should not be coasted into carelessly.

Perhaps you're thinking, *Oh, I don't even expect to marry this boy; I'm just having fun with him.* If that is the case, you should run from the relationship all the faster. Love is not something to play around with. Hearts are not like toys we can play with and then put away when we're finished. They get all wrapped up and stuck up with romance like a child's chewing gum on a teddy bear. Girls who carelessly let their emotions run free will get hurt.

Conservative Christians tend to have strict rules about what is appropriate regarding a man and woman being alone together and relating closely. Sometimes we may feel the rules are too strict and wish we could do away with some of the self-conscious reserve. However, we have to be honest with the fact that illicit relationships begin with emotional attachments. Personal sharing and one-on-one conversations are intended to bond a man and a woman. Save bonding experiences for a special relationship with a specific young man. This includes text messaging as well as real-life interaction. You have no obligation to engage with a young man who initiates chatty text conversations. Topics such as, "You know what I thought when I met you?" "What did you think when you met me?" "How are you feeling today?" are inappropriate for people who are not in a relationship. Praying together is another danger area: praying for each other is emotionally bonding and probably not a good idea outside of an official relationship. If you need to ask someone to pray about something in your life, ask your girlfriends.

There aren't always straightforward answers for what constitutes proper behavior in a given situation. What is considered appropriate varies with church groups and communities. At times you may realize you have unwittingly crossed an understood boundary. Don't panic. Just move on and don't repeat your mistake. Don't live in such fear of making a wrong move that you can't be yourself and can barely look at a young man, but be sensitive to what is considered appropriate in your community. You may think your community's standard is exceptionally old-fashioned and restrictive, but you cannot remake it, so don't fight it. There may come a day when you will even agree with it.

More than being obsessed with monitoring and analyzing your behavior, focus on keeping your heart in the right place. If your heart desires to behave appropriately, your actions will follow your heart. If you struggle to keep your heart in the right place, make yourself accountable to someone. Ask God to help you. Find more appropriate ways to satisfy the longings of your heart. If you feel too confused to evaluate whether your behavior with boys is appropriate, ask someone you trust to evaluate you. Girls can be pretty bad at judging themselves but pretty good at judging each other. Just don't be offended when your sisters or your friends tell you the truth!

FLIRTING

Does this word make you want to hold your hands over your ears and run from the room? We tend to hear a lot about it—especially as a caution to outgoing young women—but we may still feel confused about exactly what flirtatious behavior includes. Flirting is "behaving as though attracted to or trying to attract someone." Flirtatious behavior seeks to draw attention or convey a message of attraction. *I think you're a great guy. I'd like to get to know you better.* Or *Hey, here I am! Did you notice I'm here?*

When you sashay across a room full of boys, are you subconsciously trying to be noticed? Are you hoping for attention when you laugh a little too often or loudly? Are you trying to be the funniest girl in the conversation? If you are honest, figuring out your motives shouldn't be too hard.

Flirting is not a personality. Some perceptions of what constitutes flirting seem to be unfairly biased against more naturally outspoken women. A talkative and friendly young woman who is comfortable talking to young men is not a born flirt who must undergo a complete makeover of her personality. Likewise, the quiet girl in the corner has not been born without the capability to flirt. The friendly girl might not be flirting. The quiet girl might be flirting.

Outgoing women indeed need to be in control of themselves. They likely struggle most with knowing when enough is enough. However, they are the ones who keep conversations flowing and help things feel relaxed and comfortable. Quieter women can appreciate more talkative women. It would be awkward if everyone sat around in silence. Unfortunately, it seems that accusations of flirtatious behavior often spring from the jealousy of quieter women. An insecure girl may secretly wish she could be like the self-confident girl who isn't afraid to talk to the boys. So she starts some juicy gossip that draws attention to that girl's behavior and may turn others against her. Such behavior is not right or fair.

Quiet young women can flirt without making much noise. They may watch a young man to an inappropriate extent or make sure they are always near him. They might unwisely send a text or a note to a young man. Flirting can be a problem for any young woman, and probably every girl is guilty to some extent at some point in her life.

For this reason, I encourage you not to look around to notice and discuss who might be behaving flirtatiously: you could be wrong about the motives of others, and while focusing on them, you could ignore the symptoms of your own heart. Remember, this is not so much about obsessing over your behavior as having your heart in the right place. What is inside will come out. Your conduct should be becoming to the godliness you claim.

Chapter Five

Emotional Purity

"What is emotional purity?" a group of girls asked me. "Like, people use that term, and we read it in books. But what is it really?" I mentally flipped through my brain files and didn't find an answer that satisfied me immediately. What's the definition, anyway? I gave them a short answer; here's the long one.

It may be easier to explain what it isn't. Emotional impurity could be compared to having a sexual relationship with someone you're not married to. Just as we need boundaries to protect us from inappropriate physical involvement, we need boundaries to prevent us from inappropriate emotional attachments. Your feelings should not be tied up with a man who is not your boyfriend or husband.

This includes recreational dating, pre-dating, uncontrolled crushing, and playing the "we're just friends" game. A variation of being "just friends" might be "oh, we're cousins" or connected in some other way—maybe your moms were best friends growing up or whatever; it seems there are many reasons a boy and girl can be special friends that make it okay. Or maybe not. I am not discounting special relationships among members of the same family. But there is danger of inappropriate emotional attachments that can be ignored because you know you wouldn't marry.

Sharing your heart and large amounts of time with a young man whom you are not dating will lead to emotional attachment. That's just the way we're made. Sharing leads to attachment. Emotional impurity could include trying to generate a little romance with every young man who catches your eye. It's a bit like loitering around a candy store, stealing some candy every time the cashier isn't looking. You're getting little bits of something sweet that doesn't belong to you and doesn't truly satisfy. And you'll never feel good about that stolen candy because your enjoyment is illegitimate.

Women are especially susceptible to romantic involvement because we are so emotional and irresistibly attracted to romance. A young men can easily defraud a young woman emotionally, thinking they are just having a good time and not understanding how deeply involved the young woman is. It seems that invariably girls fall the hardest and get hurt the most. Young men should be taught not to take advantage of girls this way; however, girls must take responsibility for protecting themselves. Guard your own heart; no one else can do it for you. Say no to relationships without boundaries. He is not your boyfriend if he hasn't asked to date you. Contrary to how it may feel, refusing to be an "easy" girl will not ruin your chances of getting married.

Texting and private messaging is a potentially dangerous way for young men and women to connect. It is easy to share more intimately than you would face-to-face and to communicate secretly, avoiding accountability in the relationships. The safest policy for young women is not to privately message a young man at all unless perhaps it is strictly business. If a young man tries to start a text conversation with you, it is perfectly acceptable for you to simply reply, "I'm sorry. I don't text boys."

If you wonder whether you are too deeply involved with a young man, consider the amount of time you put into the relationship. If you stand in corners talking privately or text each other regularly, the sheer amount of time put into that one young man is a red flag. Surely your heart is involved.

Perhaps the relationship does not feel wrong to you because "he's my brother's friend" or "he's my cousin." Even if you have no thought of marrying him, you would probably have to admit that you enjoy the rush of the emotional connection. Both of you could be inappropriately satisfying desires for romance with each other. The fact that you feel sure you would never marry each other can blind you to the reality of what is going on.

Use caution in what you share with young men. Some things are not appropriate for sharing with someone you are not dating. Telling a young man how you're feeling or what you're worried about is not a good idea. Communicating your needs will bind you emotionally. He will probably want to help, and you will enjoy his concern. The same is true in the opposite direction. If a young man shares his struggles with you, likely your pity will be aroused, and you may be drawn into sympathy for him. Girls often find themselves uncannily attracted to troubled young men whom "no one else understands." It may be very appealing to think you could fill a unique need in his life, but this is an emotionally dangerous position. You are not the person to help him.

Consider whether it would be okay to relate to this young man in this way if you were married to someone else. Would your husband mind? Would his wife mind if he were married? If the answer is yes, you're crossing lines. Appropriate boundaries are much the same whether you're married or unmarried.

Your head needs to take over your heart, not the other way around. Your feelings may scream romantic vibes so loudly that you believe them, but your feelings have no base in reality. How can you know what an informal friendship means to a young man? It's an awkward question to ask. *Hey, I love being friends, but are you feeling platonic or romantic?* That conversation is unlikely to happen.

Many young women have assumed a young man had a particular interest in her when he was just enjoying no-strings-attached interaction. Young women can give men false hopes in this way as well. I recall a young woman from my youth who hung on the sidelines chatting vivaciously with a boy younger than herself who was clearly over the moon for her. The rest of us looked on askance at her behavior. Later, he sent her roses, and she let the whole world know she had no idea why the silly boy had done such a thing. I can only imagine his crushing humiliation.

Romantic relationships need clear boundaries, defined beginnings—and endings, if necessary. Marriage is not something to drift into. It is a lifetime covenant that will be most secure with clear boundaries both before and after the wedding.

CRUSHES

A crush is defined as "a brief and intense infatuation with someone, especially someone unattainable." It's that unrequited feeling you may imagine to be love toward a young man you admire but in reality is just an intense attraction. A crush can produce powerful emotions, making something that exists only in your head feel very real. It is a form of fantasy because it has no reality in real life. It is not true love because there is no attachment, no growth in the relationship, and no learning to know one another better. You may view crushing as a harmless activity, something to do for fun, but it is not as harmless as you think.

Crushes can make young women do foolish things; an otherwise sensible young woman may be drawn into flirtatious behavior if she allows her feelings to run wild. The intensity of a crush may lead a young woman to believe the feeling will last forever, but a crush seldom materializes into something more. Even if it should, you would not want to look back on your earlier foolish behavior with embarrassment.

Crushes tend to be fleeting and fickle. You may feel like the one you have right now is the real thing and will last forever, but take a minute to flip back through your crush history. A few girls claim to live life untroubled by strong temptations to crush, but many of us know what it's like to have a trail of crushes. *When I was in the fifth grade, I liked Ethan; I thought he was so funny. William came to our school in seventh grade, and all the girls were in love with his beautiful eyes. When I started going with the youth, I liked Joel—until he started dating someone else. Then I went to Bible School and met Peter. He was a lot of fun, and I kind of expected him to ask me—but he never did. There's Lucas, who I met at street meetings; he is so good-looking and seems so spiritual, but I don't know if I'll ever see him again.* Isn't this how it can go?

Proverbs 4:23 encourages us to keep our hearts with all diligence. *Keep* as used here has the connotation of guarding or maintaining. Our hearts don't know what they want and need.

They get all mixed up and try to wander out on their own. We need to keep an eye on them and tell them what to do, not the other way around. Can you feel like a whole and happy woman without nurturing a crush in your heart? Being consumed by crushes is an indication of inner empty places we should be filling with other things: the pursuit of God, relationships with others, and service.

If you find yourself struggling in relation to young men, whether it be flirting, pre-dating, or secret crushing, here are a few things that may help you.

- Focus on your relationship with God. I don't mean that you should try to work up an exciting devotional experience, but seriously consider whether your life is pleasing to him and how you could serve him better.
- Find meaning in service. Instead of living for the next good time, notice the needs of others and take opportunities to meet those needs.
- Talk to someone if you struggle with flirting or crushing, preferably your mom or another older woman—someone who will help you and not tease you. Discussing these things with girls your age is generally unwise; it can make nonexistent relationships feel more real and increase your struggle.
- Understand that a romantic relationship would *not* meet all your needs—even marriage would not do that. No man can fill the giant holes of neediness in a woman's heart. We need to find our security in Christ.
- Focus on healthy relationships with women, both younger and older. Developing closer relationships with women helps to fill our hearts so that we aren't

so consumed by inappropriate thoughts and behavior toward boys.

- Work on relationships in your home. Improving relationships with your parents and siblings will help to fill empty places in your heart. The way you relate to your family also sets the tone for how you will relate to others for the rest of your life, so get in some good practice.
- Finally, if you don't feel rebellious toward God's boundaries and you sincerely want to do what's right, you do not need to worry much about whether you're behaving appropriately. This may sound simplistic after all that I've said, but conscientious young women can over-focus on their every word and action and become awkward in relationships; I don't want that to happen to you. Remember that our behavior springs from our hearts. Focus on keeping your heart in the right place.

EMOTIONAL PURITY IN DATING

Until the day you marry, there are physical and emotional boundaries in a dating relationship as well. Just because he is your boyfriend does not mean he is entirely yours. Oversharing emotionally could include sharing too freely and too early in a dating relationship—for example, saying, "I love you" too soon. There are layers of intimacy that need to build organically for true romance. Enjoy each level and allow your relationship to progress naturally to a deeper level.

Having boundaries in your physical relationship is important, but you may not be as aware that you need boundaries in your discussions. Couples have been tempted into sin by too-intimate conversations. Deepening sharing is appropriate during an engagement, but you still can't talk about everything. Discussing sexual temptations, questions, or fears is unwise. Find someone else to talk to about these things. If you must share something like this—for example, confessing sexual failure—it should be done with the involvement of others; someone else should at least know you're having the conversation.

A dignified, self-confident young woman has a bit of reserve. Let your boyfriend initiate moves into deeper territory; don't rush him with hints and suggestions. Let him say "I love you" first. Let him propose without hints that now would be a good time, even if he has a more passive personality. If you push him around before you are married, I think you may someday hate him for letting you do it after you're married. Even after you're engaged, you need some reserve. It's not appropriate for you to tell him everything you think of him or to be too cozily aggressive with physical proximity. Save some things for after the wedding. You will have a lifetime together to express your passion if God wills.

Never forget that boundaries are always for your benefit; they are not there to spoil your fun. Emotional purity is as important as physical purity. If you feel discouraged by temptations and failures, be comforted that we are faulty humans; we don't always know or do the right thing. This is not about perfection but about learning and growing in character. Learning to restrain your emotions is essential for developing the loveliness of the girl inside.

Chapter Six

Fantasy World

One important area of inward loveliness is purity in thought. Where do your thoughts go when you let them wander at will? When you're alone? Tired? Sad? Bored? It is not uncommon for young women to become trapped in romantic or sexual daydreams. This may seem harmless, especially if no one knows about them and you have no intentions of acting on them.

The fantasy may center on someone you know, imagining what it would be like to date him or be married to him. It's not hard for a young woman with a moderate amount of imagination and normal emotions to project herself into a fantasy love life, a wedding day, or a honeymoon. *If no one knows about it, it's not hurting anything, is it?*

Maybe you fantasize about someone you don't know. *Isn't that better?* The handsome, friendly man with the heart-stopping smile who came into the place of business where you work today. *Did he think I'm cute? Is he married? What if he had said... and I had said...*

Maybe you fantasize about someone completely fictitious. *That has to be better. It's not as if I'll ever be tempted to act it out if he isn't even real.* Maybe your daydreams are fueled by your reading, and you are the lucky heroine until you close the book and sigh regretfully, finding yourself still alive in a dull and loveless existence. The book is ended, but perhaps you write a sequel in your head.

Are fantasies just a harmless pastime, a way to entertain and amuse yourself? Do they really matter, since no one knows what you're thinking?

FANTASY EXPOSED

There are serious problems with fantasy, whether or not you know the hero, or whether the relationship is merely romantic or crossing into sexual. For one, fantasy is not real life. When you live in a fantasy world, things happen as you wish. You are the queen of your universe. Every time you entertain a fantasy, you slip out of real life into a world of your own making. The more you do this, the harder it is to engage in and cope with your own real, imperfect life.

Another problem is that the line between reality and unreality will become increasingly blurred; you will find it difficult to tell yourself the truth about any situation. You cannot permanently move into your fantasy world. You are always forced back to some level of reality. Investing in the real world and learning how to cope with its disappointments and imperfections is important.

Women may tend to engage in milder forms of sexual fantasy than men—though not always—and for this reason, they may imagine their fantasies to be less harmful. However, fantasy is fantasy. A diet of romance novels and romantic daydreams is comparable to the temptations of pornography, a type of sexual fantasy men commonly find themselves drawn to. Both are an escape from reality. Both fuel desires that cannot be satisfied, so that they increase frustration and emotional emptiness. Both are a form of impurity. Lust is not only found in rawer forms; a craving for romance is a form of lust.

I once heard a young woman say that it does not matter if she reads romance novels because she understands the men portrayed in them are not realistic. This is not a logical justification. A man may be quite aware that pornographic stars are not portrayed realistically, but that does not make it okay for him to view pornography. In both cases, the unrealism is what draws the consumer. The unreality of fantasy is a problem, no matter the content.

You may tell yourself your fantasies are completely harmless. However, would you be okay with your "harmless" daydreams being wirelessly broadcasted onto a screen where others could read them or emailed to someone like an internet accountability report? If you shrink from such a thought, your fantasies are not so innocent.

What about truly dark fantasies? Maybe you have no idea where some of your awful thoughts come from and don't even know how to describe them. Some young women may feel trapped in vicious cycles of fantasies they don't even invite. Don't collapse under the weight of guilt and shame; you are not a hopeless case. Fantasies are often a subconscious barometer of traumas, misconceptions, and undealt-with struggles. Your temptations of the mind likely reveal areas of need and struggle in your life. Consider what type of fantasies tempt you. What seems to prompt them? What do they reveal about the part of your life that needs attention? Focusing on the problem itself is frustrating without considering your life as a whole. Our lives are not divided up into non-connected segments. We cannot fix them piece by piece. Sharing your struggles with someone may help you to figure out what prompts your thoughts.

Consider whether you are permitting yourself an indulgence in some area. For women, this is often in the area of reading material. You can't indulge in sensual literature and be truly surprised to struggle with inappropriate thoughts. If you have seen or read something in the past that keeps returning to your mind, make an effort to think of better things and allow that memory to dim rather than keeping it alive in your mind.

Girls who have been molested or exposed to things they should not have may find their thoughts affected by these events. If you are hiding something that has happened to you, tell someone about it. Being freed from your past will help you in your mind struggles.

LIVING IN REALITY

If you regularly struggle with fantasy, consider what aspect of reality you try to escape. We all struggle to accept reality on some level: life is not easy, and sometimes challenging things come our way. In the real world, things seldom happen exactly as we wish. People do not say and do the "right" things. They let us down sometimes. Even in a romantic relationship, you will discover that your boyfriend or husband will not be perfect. He won't always follow the script you have in mind. This is why fantasy is terrible preparation for marriage. Learn to cope with the bad and sad and hard things in your life. As you learn how to deal with reality by staying in it and navigating tough spots successfully, you will find your drive to escape is reduced.

Reality can be painful for sensitive people, those who have been hurt and have not been taught to cope well with emotional pain. Just being alive may feel difficult some days, but no one is doomed to a life of miserable reality. Jesus died to free us from every kind of bondage and equip us with all we need to serve him joyfully. It may take some time, but you can learn to cope with the difficulties and disappointments of everyday life.

An essential aspect of living in reality—rather than avoiding it by escaping into fantasy—is learning to accept life's struggles. Train yourself to stay in reality. Pain will not kill you; permitting ourselves to feel the depths of pain enables us to feel more alive to legitimate pleasures. Teach yourself new ways of coping with disappointments. When you face something distressing, find a safe person to share with.

Journaling can be an excellent method of sorting out life and relieving feelings, even if you immediately tear up what you've written or delete the document. Write whatever comes to mind at the moment. If you tend to be unemotional, allowing yourself to express your feelings in a good cry might be very helpful. Don't be afraid to feel sad. It is normal and okay to feel sad sometimes.

And don't forget to pray. God can be reached anytime, from anywhere. If it's 2:00 a.m., he is not asleep. If you're away from home, he's still with you. You don't even need to pick up your phone to contact him. Isn't that marvelous!

Remind yourself that your longings cannot all be filled on earth. Life has its happy times, but complete fulness of joy will only be experienced in the perfection of heaven. For now, we live in a shadow of that joy, experiencing glimpses of it. A fantasy world may feel like creating our heaven, but it is only a poor and unsustainable imitation the devil tries to trick us with. We cannot make heaven for ourselves. We have to learn how to live on earth to go to heaven. In heaven, everything *will* be perfect.

Don't make the mistake of assuming that a romantic or sexual relationship will cure your struggles. It might soothe them temporarily but won't be a complete solution. As reality settles in with a real-life relationship, you may find your temptations growing worse. Address your struggles now. Getting married will not fix your problems.

If you are struggling with fantasy, confide in a mature person you can trust. Confession helps to break down the shame of secrecy and brings healing relief. Having someone to encourage us and hold us accountable gives us incentive to fight against temptation. Opening our lives to others is scary, but it is a huge step into the reality we need. Relationships help reconnect us to our feelings and offer support as we deal with real life. We need the love and accountability of a church family.

God calls Christians to engage with each other, to love and serve each other. Fantasy is all about ourselves and can only be categorized as selfish. In a fantasy, you are not learning how to be a good daughter and sister or future girlfriend and wife. You distance yourself from the people right beside you when you go away in your head to a fantasy place. You do not learn how to relate to people who disappoint you because in your fantasy they never do. Growing and relating to others is crucial to successful and healthy Christian living. The girl inside needs to be firmly anchored in reality to thrive.

Chapter Seven

How You Feel

God created women with lots of emotion and feelings, so this must be good. However, we do need to learn to control our emotions and not let them run away with us. Emotions can change without warning. They can take over our feelings without permission. They can keep us in a state of confusion.

Emotions are feelings caused by situations, such as triggered memories, interaction with people, things people say, or your physical state—for example, being exhausted. Sometimes we don't know why we suddenly cry and feel like we've lost our last friend. We may feel like singing or bursting into hysterical laughter. Emotions try to do their own thing sometimes.

This can seem to apply more to some personalities, but it is probably only true outwardly. Restrained people feel plenty of emotions; they just keep a tighter lid on them. A quiet, seemingly calm girl might have emotions that fluctuate just as violently those of a more outgoing, obviously emotional girl—in fact, she may feel them even more keenly because they are less expressed. The quiet, shy person in the corner who may seem boring probably has a very colorful inner life.

Anger, fear, disgust, joy, sadness, surprise, and contempt are the seven basic emotions.[1] These feelings are a normal part of being human. We are not flawed if we experience strong or fluctuating emotions—that is a sign of emotional health. Being locked in unshakeable feelings of sadness and despair or feeling frozen and emotionless are signs of depression. Our emotions should respond naturally to the stimuli of living. Laughing and crying are signs of good emotional health. Even anger, although it should not be allowed to control us, is healthier than complete apathy.

The trick is not to let emotions rule our lives. Even though we cannot help the emotions we experience, we can control what we do with them and what we let them do to us. We may not be able to help crying over something—and there are times we should cry, such as when grieving a death—but we do not need to regularly weep with abandon.

We laugh spontaneously when something strikes us funny. That is normal, but we do not need to continue to laugh hysterically at things that only merit a smile or giggle, not a belly laugh. This means that it may be acceptable for something to be funny in church every once in a while. But the shoulders of an entire row of youth girls don't need to quiver with suppressed mirth for whole minutes.

MANAGING EMOTION

It's easy for us to become preoccupied with how we feel. When we experience negative feelings, we tend to wonder what is wrong and desperately try to seek happy feelings. Negative emotions may be minor—loneliness or mild depression—or they can turn into a deep depression, anxiety, and possibly even suicidal thoughts. In our low times, we tend to focus inward, looking for ways to soothe our pain. We need to allow our pain to push us toward God. Rather than wallowing in unhappy feelings, tell God about them. God knows you, and he knows how you feel. Tell yourself the truth. Instead of telling yourself that you have a terrible life and nothing ever goes right, think of everything you have going for you. Be realistic: *I'm depressed because I'm tired and my day was frustrating; I'll feel better in the morning.*

Sometimes people try to manage their feelings by locking them away and pretending they don't exist. Others allow their feelings to control them to the point that they lack self-restraint. Somewhere in the middle is a happy medium: being aware of but not controlled by the way you feel.

Repressing your feelings is not a solution; it is not possible to stop having emotions. All you're doing is ignoring them. This becomes very stressful. Acknowledge your feelings and deal with them appropriately. Don't blame others for your problems. We all have imperfect homes and bad experiences; we grow up with those imperfections sticking to us, plus new ones of our own. Granted, some people have more challenging experiences than others, and we do not understand why things happen as they do. But none of us can use our past as an excuse for anything. Christ died for all of us. His grace is equally available to us. Women who have been seriously wronged can become some of the sweetest, most caring people.

What about persistent negative feelings? Maybe you feel stuck in sadness. Perhaps you're struggling with loneliness or despair you can't shake off. Unhappiness is not something we can altogether avoid; life was never intended to be one continuous party. Our life on earth is incomplete. Sometimes we're disappointed. Sometimes we hurt. Sometimes the weight of being alive feels like too much. You are not crazy when you feel this way. The apostle Paul describes the entire creation groaning and travailing together as we wait for full redemption (Romans 8:18-27). There are not enough chocolates, specialty coffee drinks, or fuzzy blankets to fix the brokenness we feel. But we know there is more to life than the present. And we know God provides a way of salvation for us, *regardless of how we feel momentarily.* "For God so loved the world, that he gave his only begotten Son, that whosoever believeth on him should not perish, but have everlasting life" (John 3:16).

OUR PAMPERED LIVES

Life is so easy for us in many ways. We live in relative wealth and ease compared to much of the world. We have so much that we can easily be spoiled and crave more. We can get our religion mixed up with the American dream so that we come to believe a version of the health-and-wealth gospel: I'm a good Christian, so God ought to make everything pleasant for me.

Our comforts and conveniences shelter us from true hardship and shield us from many brutal realities. If we lived in poverty amidst death and bloodshed, operating daily in basic survival mode, we would have a different mindset. We are used to top-of-the-line medical care, with a pill for pretty much everything. We are protected from pain and discomfort as much as possible. We're so used to fixing things that we can be too quick to turn to sleep aids or depression medication. We don't know what to do with our sadness.

We can get confused by the incorrect concept that the Christian life is supposed to be all happiness. God asks us to do un-fun things like serving others, sacrificing our desires, and taking up our crosses. (Luke 9:23). The Bible frequently mentions the hardships of being a Christian. But we can spend a lot of time feeling insulted and let down if we're unhappy and life doesn't go the way we want it to. Christians do experience joy and happiness; it just doesn't come by getting our own way. The paradox of joy is that we have to give up in order to receive.

Jesus did not have a happy, carefree life—certainly not during the years of his earthly ministry. He had no home. He was hated so much that he was crucified, betrayed by someone who was supposed to love him. He suffered intensely to give up his will in the Garden of Gethsemane. Many followers of Christ have been persecuted and martyred. Where do we get the idea that we deserve to have a happy, comfortable life? We are not saved to a fun and easy life; we are saved to serve and sometimes to suffer. God does not owe us any happiness. He does not owe us anything. But he freely offers peace, love, and grace enough for anything.

It may help you to learn more about current Christian martyrs. Reading about persecuted and martyred Christians makes our troubles look insignificant. Becoming angry with God for not fixing aspects of our lives we don't like is petty. God loves a persecuted Christian woman in Russia or Indonesia, yet he does not prevent her from suffering. The full reward is yet to come for both of us.

In modern America, most of us do not suffer for our faith, or even from serious financial difficulties. How do we deny ourselves and take up our crosses when we have fun events to attend, reliable vehicles at our disposal, and an abundance of physical comforts, plus most of our wants?

Small choices of self-denial can be surprisingly difficult. Maybe it's the choice between going out with your friends or staying home to help your parents. Perhaps it's giving up your time to stay with siblings so your parents can have a date. It could mean choosing a device that costs hundreds of dollars less and giving more money in the offering basket. It might mean spending less on eating out, clothing, or expensive hobbies, maybe because you're doing voluntary service work or teaching school instead of getting a higher-paying job. It might be as tiny as sacrificing some me-time to play with children or read to them. It might be putting extra effort into visiting grandparents or other older people or helping busy mothers. Don't think you'll have more time for such things at any other time in your life. Choosing to drag ourselves out of our misery and do something for someone can make us surprisingly happy.

OTHER REASONS YOU MAY FEEL BAD

Maybe you feel depressed because of wrongdoing. Perhaps you said something unkind or told a sort-of lie, and you're trying not to think about it because you hate apologizing. It would be much better to spend an awkward minute apologizing than to be miserable for days or months or years.

Maybe something happened between you and someone else that you should talk about. Perhaps you accidentally saw or read something that bothers your conscience, or you deliberately chose to do something you knew was wrong. Confess it to someone. Keeping your conscience free contributes to your happiness and peace of mind. One young woman used the expression "dumping her junk." We all need a place to dump our junk sometimes.

We're taught to be good girls to a fault. We feel like we have to live above all real sin, so that when we fall, it may seem better to hide it than to expose it. After all, what will people think? Good girls just don't do things like that! The fact is, none of us are exempt from sin. We all do things we shouldn't do sometimes, and sometimes they're just plain embarrassing. But we're all normal. It's a lot easier to just admit our normality to each other. Everyone needs someone with whom they can share their foolish and embarrassing moments and not be judged.

Sometimes our unhappiness may come from simply being self-absorbed. It's far too easy to focus on ourselves and our own needs and desires. Self-focus nurtures discontent and unhappiness. Learn to look beyond yourself and notice others' needs. Were you so unhappy about missing an event that you didn't notice how you could have helped your mother, how tired your father was, or how quiet your sister was at the supper table?

Modern young people are often accused of being narcissistic—self-centered and selfish. This may or may not be fair or accurate. Being self-absorbed has always been a problem for humans. But it is true that today's youth do not face some of the hardships that people did in the past. Our easy lives can insulate us from true need and care for others. Take the initiative to be involved in any opportunities available: street meetings, soup kitchens, missions, vacation Bible school, children's church, or just reach out personally in your neighborhood. Look for ways to break the barriers of your privileged horizons. Learning to be aware of others' needs and giving your time and energy to serve is probably the best thing you can do for your emotional equilibrium.

Remember to tell yourself God's truths, regardless of how you feel. Feelings are just feelings; they are not a reliable indication of reality. Take charge of them so they don't take control of you.

Chapter Eight

Your Cycle

You may wonder what your monthly cycle has to do with anything. It has much to do with your feelings, so let's talk about this. Getting old enough to have a period involves much more than just figuring out how to deal with the bleeding. It's easy to focus on dealing with one week out of the month and not realize what else is happening all month. Understanding what's going on in your body the entire month can save you—and those around you—a lot of grief.

Female hormones are constantly busy. Our hormones change throughout the entire month, rising and falling in a natural rhythm. Your body prepares for ovulation and the possibility of pregnancy every month, and undoes the preparations when you do not conceive. Your body is constantly winding up or gearing down; no wonder this background work affects our feelings.

You may be frustrated to feel different from one day to the

next. One day you may feel great and energetic; the next, it's hard to get going. One day your mood is light and buoyant; the next, you feel depressed. Feeling this way is normal, and there isn't much we can do about it.

I'm not a gynecologist, so I can't explain to you exactly what which hormones are doing when, but your cycle follows a predictable pattern each month in which various hormones do their thing. Your body is constantly changing, affecting your thoughts, moods, energy levels, creativity, confidence, and even the way your brain works. Not understanding this can lead to frustration. You may panic when you feel exhausted and low-spirited. You might think you're going crazy—or more likely, everyone else is going crazy—when you're experiencing PMS (premenstrual syndrome) right before your period arrives. Everything can seem overwhelming and terrible, and things you can overlook at other times of the month can be unbearably annoying.

The more aware you are of where you are in your cycle and the way it affects you, the more you can take control of your feelings. You don't have to be like an erratic kite, soaring high one day and swooping low the next. A little self-awareness and personal grace can make a difference.

THE SEASONS OF YOUR CYCLE

The four parts of a woman's cycle are often compared to the four seasons.

- Winter is when you are menstruating, that is, having your period. The first day of your period is day one of your cycle. Winter lasts approximately days one through six.

- Spring is approximately days seven through thirteen. This is the pre-ovulation stage when your body shifts from having a period—undoing preparations for pregnancy—to gearing up for ovulation and the possibility of pregnancy again.
- Summer is approximately days fourteen through twenty-one. You will ovulate sometime during this season; this is the time of the month you are able to become pregnant.
- Fall is approximately days twenty-two through twenty-nine. Your body winds down from the "high" of ovulation and prepares for you to have another period.

You may not always notice a distinct change from day to day, but you will notice patterns in mood changes. Tracking your period, even journaling how you feel during your seasons, can help you feel much more in control of your life. If you understand "that's just getting on my nerves because my period is due tomorrow," you can remain calm and not make a big issue out of something that wouldn't be an issue during your summer. When you don't understand what's happening, you may feel out of control, getting easily upset and saying things you later regret.

During winter, you likely feel less energetic. You will likely sleep more and be less enthusiastic about physical activities. You will probably have some pain with cramping the first day or two, making you feel like taking it easy. Our culture encourages women to carry on full steam ahead during every phase of their cycle. The sanitary products available to us make it possible for us to carry on normally and discreetly with no one being the wiser. We can also take painkillers to mitigate the discomforts, but taking too much medication is not a good thing. If you suffer severe pain or if you must attend a big event during this time, you may need painkillers, but normal period cramping on a day we're not super-busy is manageable. It's a reminder to take it a little easy while your body is in this season.

Emotionally, you might feel blah, not necessarily depressed or stressed but lethargic and uninspired. You might prefer reading in bed with a hot cup of tea to socializing; this is okay. Getting your period is normal and healthy; it is not a sickness or weakness, and it doesn't mean you can't do anything. However, it is wise to know your limits and not overtax your body. It is not the time to exhaust yourself with strenuous exercise or stay up half the night if you can at all help it.

While we cannot just take a vacation every time we're menstruating, it is sensible to do what we can to reduce our stress and workload. You may have to go to work as usual, but you don't have to go to the volleyball game that evening. It is a better time to catch up on sewing than to go on an all-day shopping trip. Sometimes big events fall over this time, and you have no choice but to exert yourself. If this happens to you, take it a little easier the next day or two and be sure to get enough sleep. Running high on caffeine or adrenaline the entire month is not wise and will lead to abnormal fatigue. Powering through menstruation at high speed will deplete you for the rest of your cycle. Your body is in a resting, cleansing mode.

In the spring of your cycle, you will feel energy returning, and if you have not exhausted yourself during your winter, you will likely feel inspired about life and have many ideas. Spring is a good time to plan and catch up on little things you've been neglecting. It's a good time to tackle big projects, like deep cleaning or painting.

Summer is generally the favorite part of a woman's cycle. It is when you feel the most outgoing and energetic, so it is a good time to be with friends and attend social events. You feel at ease and can overlook little things that might annoy you at other times. You may be too excited to get deeply involved in creative outlets because your mind is full of enthusiasm and new ideas. Enjoy your summer, but don't panic when it ends. It will come again.

Fall is often the least favorite part of a woman's cycle, especially the end of it. You may feel confused, depressed, emotional, or even like you're going crazy. Keep in mind that it *is* you going crazy, not the whole world! This is when you tend to have relationship struggles. Your family's quirks and bad habits, which you may be able to overlook during your summer, may become super-annoying. Scientific research even suggests there's a reason that noise bothers us more during this time. Instead of dwelling on the eccentricities of your parents or the brattiness of your siblings, remind yourself that you are the one in a bad mood. Take a deep breath. Spend time alone if you can. Fall is a good time to delve into creative passions; we are often most creative and can concentrate intensely at this time of the month. Talk politely with your family about your frustrations if you need to, but don't weep and rage about the house, spreading desolation and ruin in everyone's day. This, too, shall pass.

DEALING WITH PMS

PMS, premenstrual syndrome, is a specific term for the mood and body changes a woman experiences the week before her period. The hormonal changes in your body that make you moody and irritable may also make you feel bloated and experience food cravings. You may not sleep as well. This is normal.

However, severe PMS or severe bleeding and cramping during your period may indicate a health problem. Try to alleviate it with things like an improved diet and better lifestyle habits.

I do not recommend the birth control pill to try to correct problems with your cycle. Gynecologists commonly suggest this as a solution, but it stops the best parts of your cycle as well as the worst, and further confuses your body. As I understand it, the pseudo periods you get while on the Pill are not natural cycles but hormone-manipulated bleeding. The Pill works by suppressing ovulation, which may temporarily relieve some of your symptoms, but it is in no way fixing anything. Take good care of yourself and your cycle if you want a healthy life and the option of bearing children someday.

PMS is real, but it doesn't mean you get to sulk, cry, and take out your feelings on everyone else. Learn not to take yourself too seriously. Your life is not in ruins—it only feels like it. Be quiet if you can't say anything nice. Cry behind a closed door. Blow your nose and get on with life. Make yourself a cup of tea. Read a book. Listen to quiet music. Go to bed early. It may feel like the universe is blowing apart inside you, but that's just how you feel today. Don't base significant decisions on how you feel when experiencing PMS—trying to decide if you want to teach school again next year? Move away from home? Break up with your boyfriend? Don't decide right now. Definitely wait till after your period starts.

Hormonal balance is a delicate thing. Taking reasonably good care of your body helps to keep hormonal fluctuations from being too dramatic. Eat well and get enough sleep. Constantly wearing your body down will take a toll on your health. You may not notice some of these effects until later in life. Your body is resilient in many ways, but the systems that make it operate as it's supposed to are delicate—don't abuse the gift of good health.

Young people tend to feel invincible. You have a lot of energy. You sort of feel like you'll live forever when you're seventeen. And you may be able to accomplish a lot if you push yourself a little. A little caffeine and adrenaline can go a long way. Enjoy your energy and your abilities, but don't abuse your body. Your health is a gift from God. Your body is an amazing part of Creation. Just as God asks us to be good stewards of the rest of Creation, he wants us to take care of our bodies (1 Corinthians 6: 19, 20; Romans 12:1).

You only get one body, and broken health can be difficult to restore. Hormonal problems often become a big deal for young women after they marry and try to conceive children. There are many reasons for infertility. Not every infertile woman has abused her health. But we should realize that every aspect of our body is interconnected, and our hormonal cycles can easily be disrupted.

Your cycle is an important and precious part of your womanhood. We live in a culture that encourages women to 'sterilize' themselves with birth control, even if it messes with their hormonal health. They are encouraged to believe abortion is acceptable for the right reasons. Lesbianism and transgenderism are promoted in confusing, cleverly-disguised rhetoric that demeans women's bodies and their unique capabilities. God made you a woman. Your body is specially designed, and its capabilities are good.

Chapter Nine

Sexual Addictions

Emotional turmoil and depression can result in various unlovely inner struggles for girls. It is not uncommon for young women from conservative church settings to struggle with various sexual addictions, such as masturbation, fantasy, immoral music or literature, and sometimes pornography. It is more uncommon for them to talk about it. These struggles are deeply sensitive, secretive, and shameful and are often portrayed as male problems. Christian women can feel an extra layer of shame in revealing struggles like these. We need more openness and safety among church sisters in relating to these things. There is no shame in being human and needing support; the shame is in struggling along alone and afraid.

If you struggle with any of these things, be assured you are not the only one. There is no new sin, no woman so unique that she struggles with something no one else ever has. The devil wants to keep us bound in the shadows of secrecy, shame, and defeat. But God longs to heal us and give us a life free from condemnation. We can move from the shadows of shame into the light of forgiveness.

We are all imperfect and sexually broken in some way because of our fallen world. Even if you do not connect with any of the particular struggles I mentioned, you struggle somewhere. And as a sister in Christ, you need to offer love and support for anyone who does struggle. Don't criticize, conjecture, or gossip if someone you know confesses to failure. We all struggle in some way. We all come short of being who God wants us to be sometimes. When someone admits their dark secrets, they make themselves incredibly vulnerable. Acceptance and love are healing. Judgment is devastating. Don't think *I'd never do that.* If you had been in her shoes, you probably would have. And likely you have failed in something just as wrong, though you may not realize it. We all need God's light to illuminate our hearts.

FINDING FREEDOM

If you struggle in one of these areas, you may feel defensive. You may wonder whether your sin really condemns you. After all, you keep up a pretty good Christian life outwardly. No one knows about it. You're not hurting anyone. You'll stop soon. You'll give yourself a little more time. You'll wait till it's easier to get help. We can have a warped mindset in which we see invisible sins as somehow less urgent than visible ones.

If you have not stopped yet, don't deceive yourself by thinking that you will or can stop on your own. Waiting will not make it easier. The longer you put off getting help, the deeper these habits become entrenched, and the more difficult it becomes to say, "I need help."

Strangely enough, we experience a lot of reluctance to give up our sexual sins. We do these things because they feel good at the time. They are familiar and comforting and offer false security. We like them a lot, even though we hate them a lot. We may be afraid to lose these comforts because we don't believe God can replace them with something better.

We need to tell ourselves the truth, loud and clear. We need to read the truth in God's Word, hear it from those who care about us, write it and speak it to ourselves until our hearts follow our heads.

- God is not out to take good things away from us.
- God is good; he is for us, not against us.
- God wants a better life for you; his plan for you just probably doesn't look like the plan you have for you.
- Abandon what you think you want and throw yourself onto his mercy: "Here I am. I don't know how to be what you want me to be. I don't even know if I want to be good, but I want you."

Maybe you're clinging to shreds of self-justification, unwilling to use the word *sin* for your struggle.

- The Bible doesn't seem to speak particularly to my struggle.
- I'm not hurting anyone else.
- I'm not hurting myself.
- I deserve gratification.
- I'll stop when I get married.

Whether or not you can find a particular sexual habit specifically denounced in scripture, you can find principles that apply: Sexual sins are self-centered and encourage us in selfish and undisciplined behavior. Continuing in them will prevent us from developing the servant behavior God wants us to develop. We are not thinking of others, certainly not in a serving way, when we engage in immoral behavior—we are thinking only of ourselves. We become weak in other areas of self-control. Would you trust someone else whom you knew had an uncontrollable habit? Why trust yourself? Being absorbed in ourselves turns our focus inward and hinders us from noticing the needs of others, developing outward, and growing closer to others.

These habits prevent us from maturing emotionally. They are the things we fall back on when disappointed, sad, lonely, worried, or angry. We don't learn how to cope with intense feelings in a constructive way. We fear deep face-to-face sharing, vulnerability, and need. In our quest to appear strong outwardly, we may be falling apart on the inside.

You can't count on marriage to help you. In marriage, you must learn to be vulnerable and relate very closely with someone. It will not be easy if you are not already learning to connect well with others. Sexual sin is self-centered; a marriage relationship is about giving and meeting each other's needs. You may be disappointed and frustrated in marriage because your sin has established unrealistic expectations. Married people may well find their old temptations staring them in the face—if not immediately, when the going gets a little challenging. The time to deal with temptations is now.

I know it's embarrassing and hard, and you just want it to go away. You're supposed to be a good girl who knows better, which increases your shame. This pressure to be a good girl at all costs can prevent women from bringing their struggles to the light and finding help. Despite appearing to be good girls, they know they are bad girls. Their shame drives them deeper into the very things they want to escape. They try harder and fall farther, consumed by secrets they feel they cannot share. They may feel inferior to others, convinced that they are simply not trying as hard as everyone else. They pray and read their Bibles, and no power from heaven sweeps in and frees them.

While immorality is certainly a problem, I would like to deflect attention from the sins themselves for a moment and suggest that someone who struggles with such addictions is as much a *sad girl* as a *bad girl*. Sad girls carry pain they cannot shake, feelings they cannot express, and return to the only thing they know that offers pseudo relief. "Bad" girls need to stop mentally beating themselves up for failure and look at what makes them sad girls, what pain drives their intense temptations. Learning to cope with disappointments and accept reality is essential in learning to deal appropriately with pain. (See chapter six.)

Sexual struggles may begin with simple lust or curiosity, but an intense, ongoing battle with these sins indicates an emotional problem. Behind sexual addictions lies an intense craving for emotional connection. The addiction soothes that ache momentarily while deepening and intensifying it so that the pain is more intense and the addiction more appealing. It becomes a vicious cycle. Girls decide they will stop, but in sad and anxious moments, they repeat the scenario, vowing to stop again. They "stop" until the next time they feel overwhelmed, loathing themselves and hoping God's grace covers them in all their weakness, hoping that the next stretch of their lives brings escape.

To find victory, you must believe that what you are doing is wrong and that you need help. Even if it seems there is no way out for you, take that first step in faith and confess your struggle to someone. I love a simple phrase I discovered in the poetry of the Psalms: "In your [God's] light do we see light" (Psalm 36:9

ESV). Life in the dark is miserable, and we can't see our way out. When we open our sin to God's light, confessing to him our inability to do right and allowing others to see our struggles, his light shines onto us, and a path of escape becomes visible. In his light, other areas of our lives also improve, and we can experience complete wholeness. When struggling in a particular area, we often focus intensely on that one thing when we need wholeness and healing in many areas.

We may envision confession as a demoralizing experience. It is not easy, but it should strengthen, encourage, and comfort. Letting go, opening up, and revealing rather than concealing brings immense relief and freedom. To be known and loved as we are by God and others is the greatest security known to humanity.

When fleeing sin, we'd like to make a clean break and never fail again. For example, you may hear stories of drunkards who became convicted of their habit and never drank alcohol again. Instant victory may happen sometimes, but it is more common for victory over sin to be an intense uphill battle. If you fail, don't give up in defeat and think you can't do it. You probably will stumble and fall in your journey; this doesn't mean you can't make it to freedom and victory.

It is relatively easy to identify ways we can put guards around ourselves: being accountable to someone, using filters on our devices, or avoiding certain places and things, for example, but we need more than this. We are not simply saying no to sin; we must say yes to God. It is essential to look at the root of our struggle and identify the lies we are telling ourselves, the pain that eats away at us, and the insecurities that drive us to seek solace. We need to shift our mindset to align with the mind of God. Sexual sins are far more than a body problem. They are a struggle of heart and mind.

STEPS FOR HEALING

Conservative Christians tend to be cautious with modern psychology. We don't want to encourage people to dig around in their pasts so that they can find people to blame or excuses for being the way they are. We do not want to be involved in dubious practices that cause people to "recall" things from their past that may or may not have even happened or involve inappropriate healing practices. For this reason, I would not necessarily encourage you to seek help from professionals or a counseling organization. Sometimes a person does need professional help, but ideally, we should find support at home with people we know. What is the church for but to help us grow spiritually? There is an aspect of coming clean with people we don't know that seems better. It is easier to be far away from home spilling our guts to strangers. It takes courage to expose ourselves at home to those who know us well. But I believe deep and true healing comes from vulnerability with the people who know us best and love us most. In this way, relationships can be healed and restored, helping us find the peace and connection we crave.

There are basic counseling principles for healing that are universally true. We do need to look at our past—our past is what makes us who we are—but we don't look there to blame anyone. We may look back to identify and forgive hurts, real or perceived. But we let them go. We identify wrong thinking patterns so we can choose to replace them with new thinking patterns. We recognize our pain, and we lay down our right to justice. We need to forgive anyone who has wronged us in any way. Wrongs may include parents who were angry and abusive or who were simply preoccupied and overlooked our needs.

It may be siblings who took advantage of us in significant or insignificant ways, knowingly or unknowingly. Releasing these things frees us to move ahead with life in wholeness. We all have imperfect things in our history because we are all broken. In our brokenness, we hurt each other. But we can't cling to wrongs as justifications. We all need to claim responsibility for ourselves and find personal victory.

No matter what you've done or how long you've done it, or how defeated you feel, remember that shame does not define who you are. Christ died for your sins. He wants to put them far away and give you a clean slate. You can move forward from this moment into a new life. Trust God. Trust his people. It may look impossible, but continuing in bondage to sin is harder.

Immerse yourself in the Bible and good books, and memorize scripture. Fill your mind with good thoughts. Look around you and notice the needs of others; this will combat self-centeredness. Be constructively busy: take up a new hobby or revive an old interest. Study something that interests you. Establish new patterns for your day or your week. And whatever you do, don't give up. The Christian life is a progression of learning and growing. Give yourself time. Pick yourself up if you fail; don't allow shame to stop your quest to live free. Step from the shadows into the light and allow your life to be illuminated by God's grace.

Chapter Ten

Spiritual Nurture

What are you feeding the girl inside? Just as a baby demands food and cries out for relief from hunger, we feel soul hunger and cry for soul satisfaction. We feel pain and loneliness, desire and longing. We don't always recognize our appetites for what they are, and we sometimes seek fulfillment in wrong ways. Our fallen nature tends to gravitate toward the shallow and the sinful. Just as a baby may suck his thumb for comfort, we may soothe ourselves on something that isn't feeding us. We must take the initiative to seek ways to appropriately satisfy our spiritual needs.

If you were born in a Christian setting, you likely grew up surrounded by Bible teaching and don't remember hearing familiar Bible stories for the first time. Bible basics are just there in your mind like the English language. You do learn new things, just as you might learn a new word, but Bible knowledge is likely such a part of your psyche that it is easy for you to feel blasé about it. Teaching and preaching are available to you each Sunday, but just letting it fall on your ears is not sufficient. Vibrant Christian living is not a state of passivity in which we try to look good and do just enough to keep our parents and pastors happy; it must mean something to us. Appreciate the messages your pastors bring to you and allow them to speak to your needs. Don't allow criticism of your pastor's life or manner of presentation to cloud God's nourishment for you.

Our church should be a group of people we support and a gathering we attend faithfully. It seems fashionable to be critical of the church and leadership these days. Personal relationships with God and solitary Christianity are sometimes elevated over the input and accountability that comes with church membership. Beware of falling into this mindset. God established the church for our instruction, safety, and encouragement. Don't deceive yourself by believing you have personal, special enlightenment if you see things differently than everyone else at church. Churches are never perfect, but a group of people who try to follow God together is better than being alone.

When you criticize your church, you are, in essence, accusing yourself because you are part of it. It is like mistreating your own body. Churches are not perfect because they consist of imperfect people like you. If you do not appreciate your church, consider whether you are trying to "plug in" and do your part. The church should be where you enjoy being and where you find spiritual encouragement and refreshment. True, there are lifeless churches; however, they may be fewer and less dead than we think. Many times, we are projecting our attitudes and spiritual weaknesses onto the group. Don't criticize your church and try to change it; make an experiment of active involvement. Seek fulfillment in relating to those in your church family. Changing your attitude could make an amazing difference in your church life.

The church is not the only place we take in spiritual nourishment. We have to actively seek it for ourselves as well.

DEVOTIONAL HABITS

You've probably been taught the importance of having a daily time of Bible reading and prayer. Sometimes young women wonder if their devotional life is all that it should or could be. Some might feel guilty because they don't do it every single day. Some may do it daily, but they wonder if it's good enough, because it doesn't always feel inspirational. Maybe the Bible doesn't always hold your interest, and you struggle to keep your mind on prayer. Perhaps you're struggling with sin or doubt, and having a daily devotional time doesn't seem to help.

I do not believe God intended for Bible reading and prayer to be a chore that we dutifully cross off our mental list each day, feeling saintly if we've accomplished it and sinful if we have not. I don't think prayer should be something we labor over, only to realize our minds are wandering far away or we're falling asleep. On the other hand, it will not always be an emotional experience that tosses us to lofty heights of spirituality and gives us the power to live above sin for the next twenty-four hours.

We can be guilty of discussing personal devotions as if they are a talisman, a good-luck charm, or a good spell cast on your day. I have heard the advice, "if you get up early and have your devotions every morning, your whole day will go great." Maybe. I have had good days when I had devotions first thing in the morning, but I've also had terrible days that began immediately after I said *amen*.

There is no magic in Bible reading and prayer. It is possible that disciplining yourself to get up on time makes you feel good about your day. It is also possible that having a hard day now and then after you've had devotions is realistic. Maybe we're being tested on what we aspired to that morning in the solitude and secrecy of our hearts. Maybe God is trying to mold us into what we told him we wanted to become. Perhaps he is reminding us to turn to him for strength and not run on feelings of self-sufficiency. We shouldn't have personal devotional time merely in hopes of having a good day.

Why should we read the Bible? We may struggle with feeling like it's unimportant because we've had so much exposure to it. We are far more familiar with it than someone who converts to Christianity without knowing the Bible. It may feel like there isn't much new for us to discover. However, we all need regular exposure to the Bible because it is one of the primary ways God speaks to our hearts. We need reminders of what is in it; we can't remember everything we've been taught. We read to learn about God's character, to see what Christ has done for us, and to see ourselves as we are and what we should be. We learn from stories of faithful or unfaithful Bible characters. Exposing ourselves to God's Word is necessary; an emotional epiphany is optional. Some days we may close our Bibles merely thinking, *that's nice*. Other days we may be stunned with an answer to a problem or something profound that had never occurred to us in that way. It is unrealistic to expect to be stirred emotionally every time.

Think of your relationships with people. You spend time with them and learn to know them better without much conscious effort. Some specific encounters stand out as special: when you felt especially close to a parent, unusually understood by a sibling, or exceptionally bonded to a friend. These special times are highlights from a collection of average day-to-day experiences. God is not human, but we are. I don't think it's sacrilege to say our relationship with him is similar to other relationships.

So it's okay if you read your Bible this morning and didn't feel anything special. Maybe you felt like it was a boring section; you will come to something more profound another day. You've opened your mind to God's word, which is the most important thing.

If you've been discouraged with your devotional time, try resetting your expectations. Don't make it about conjuring up euphoric feelings and seeking elusive spiritual power. Open your soul to the power of God's truth and allow yourself to be pierced with the knowledge of what God wants for your life. His word is quick—alive, powerful, and sharper than a sword—penetrating in conviction (Hebrews 4:12).

It might seem nice to be guaranteed a devotional time that would make us feel good and give us magical power to deal with sin. But in reality, our devotional time should bring humility and conviction as we look into God's word and see that we do not come anywhere near to being what he wants, but that he loves us anyway and understands our weaknesses. Rather than leaving our devotional time feeling excited and powerful, it would be more beneficial to rise from this time with tears in our eyes, knowing that though we make a mess of things regularly, God understands. This repentance and knowledge of God's mercy will help us find victory. Oddly enough, the knowledge that God loves us *in spite of* rather than *because* provides the security we so desperately seek.

BIBLE STUDY

There are many ways to read and study the Bible. My favorite method has always been cover-to-cover, just like a novel, not in a year but at my own pace. In literary form, the Bible would be considered an anthology—a collection of various types of literature by different authors. However, this anthology has a theme like no other piece of literature: each text contributes to the grand story of the redemption of humanity.

We tend to separate the Bible a lot in our minds. Bible translators put chapter divisions to help us find our place. We distinctly separate the Old and New Testaments. We may think of books like Psalms and Revelations as standing entirely alone. We have the divisions of books of the law, the minor prophets, the gospels, and the epistles.

While the books of the Bible *are* individual works, once each in its separate scroll before the compilation of the Bible, they all fit together. The entire Bible is one big story: the struggles and heart cries of fallen humanity and the loving response of an almighty God. Reading large chunks at a time in the order they come, just as you would read any other book, provides a panoramic view of the gospel story that opens new vistas of insight and understanding of God's work with people. Read across chapter endings and beginnings sometimes. We can miss exciting connections because we always break our train of thought at the same place. It would be an excellent exercise to try reading the Bible in a year; there will probably be no better time for you than now.

Vary your method of Bible study if that appeals to you. Try a book study, a word study, or a topical study. Use a concordance and Bible dictionary. Look up cross references. Check the meanings of words in the original Greek or Hebrew. Read books that explain Middle Eastern culture and shed light on Bible practices, such as *Misreading Scripture with Western Eyes* by Brandon O'Brien and Randolph Richards. Read the Bible in another version; the English Standard Version is a good option. If you enjoy words, you may enjoy the Amplified Bible.

Sometimes we open our Bibles and our eyes fall on a verse that feels like a gift for the day; it is just what we need at that moment. But we should not always cherry-pick one verse for inspiration. Reading whole passages provides context and a more accurate understanding.

One woman told me she does not underline anything in her Bible because she wants to see new things every time she reads. Since her comment, I have noticed that I pay special attention to passages I've marked in my Bible, potentially missing other valuable points on that page. I don't mark things anymore.

Something that never fails to make the Bible more precious to me is reading about persecuted Christians who must hide their Bibles or sit in prison trying to recall scripture from memory. I don't value the Bible as they do simply because I have so much access to it: I have new Bibles and old Bibles, study Bibles, audio versions, and more than one Bible app on my phone. I can look up any version of the Bible online within minutes. Reading about a starving, mistreated woman sitting in a cold and filthy cell trying to recall scripture from memory makes me treasure the Bible I hold in my hands.

You might like to keep a devotional journal to record favorite verses, thoughts that inspire you, and questions you have. Writing things down can make something abstract more tangible and help you process ideas. It can also help you remember things better.

PRAYER

You've likely been taught to pray from a young age. You may dutifully pray through lists of people and situations that need divine intervention: people and situations you have been praying about for weeks, months, or years. You have nothing new to say about them, and nothing changes. As you labor through the list, your mind inevitably wanders; maybe you even fall asleep. This kind of prayer feels heavy and worthless. If you struggle with prayer, I suggest you stop and change something. Prayer is not intended to be a chore. Tell God how much you're struggling with knowing how to pray. Lay aside your list and instead pray about the things nagging at you and crowding into your thoughts.

Try a different time of day to pray. Or rewrite your prayer list: take off some things you put on only from a sense of duty, at least temporarily, and see what's left. Pray for only a few select items for several days. One idea is to divide a prayer list out over a week; for example, Monday, pray for family members, Tuesday for your church, Wednesday for unsaved friends, and so on. This breaks a long list down into manageable portions. It also avoids the monotony of covering every single item every day.

Remember that prayer is not only for devotional time. You can talk to God when you are worried or lonely, when you don't know what to do about a situation, when you need to talk to someone, or when you can't sleep. We don't always remember that God is closer to us than anyone else, knows more than anyone else, and has the power to do more for us than anyone else.

You may wonder if you really need to pray and read your Bible daily. Is it a sin to miss a day? We are such creatures of habit that we quickly revert to all or nothing. When we start skipping now and then, the skipping soon becomes more natural than not skipping. Therefore, it is best to be as regular as we possibly can. Remember, it is primarily about exposing yourself to God's Word and opening your heart to things he wants to show you. It is not about magical power and good feelings.

The discipline of choosing to take time for it each day is good for us and is a physical reminder of our spiritual goals. The effort we are willing to put into scheduling a regular devotional time probably reflects our general spiritual state. If we lie in bed till the last minute every morning and skip our devotional time, we should not be surprised to find ourselves struggling with defeat in other areas.

OTHER READING MATERIAL

What books are on your nightstand or saved on your digital book service? What we take into our minds influences the way we think and shapes our theology. We can be eager to take in scriptural teaching through books, maybe through online sermons or podcasts. Some conservative evangelical views seem to align closely with what we believe, but they are not always biblically sound.

We may feel there are voids in conservative literature being printed and that we are therefore justified in looking to broader circles to fill particular needs. This may be true at times. However, just because we can't find books on a specific subject from the most conservative publishing houses does not necessarily mean it's a neglected subject. We have a lot of sound teaching and preaching and are surrounded by many godly older people who are willing to answer questions and provide guidance for us. Case in point: I remember when Joshua Harris's book *I Kissed Dating Goodbye* was making waves among conservative young people. Someone said, "I don't understand it; we shouldn't need this book." We already had teaching and preaching against casual dating practices. But somehow, a book by someone else was more meaningful. In recent years, Joshua Harris left his wife and the church he pastored. He supports the homosexual and transgender community and stopped reprints of his book.

Your best advice and guidance will probably come from people right around you—people who understand you and want you to succeed. They may not have a polished delivery or a college degree, but that doesn't mean they don't know some things about Christian living.

If you enjoy devotional books, use them only as supplements with your Bible open; they are not a replacement for personal Bible reading and study. Keep in mind that the thoughts in a devotional book are simply another person's perspective; they are not a Bible translation. Consider who wrote the book. Would you go to church with that person? I have been surprised by the books my peers are devouring and promoting. We can certainly learn from people from other denominations, but reading widely should be done critically and not as spiritual, devotional-type reading. Reading is an intimate form of influence. When we read for spiritual nurture and self-help, we must constantly measure the teaching against God's Word. Just because it's labeled "Christian" doesn't mean it is doctrinally sound.

Someone pointed out an interesting phenomenon about conservative Christians: we tend to devalue literature produced by conservatives like ourselves—or, heaven forbid—even more conservative groups. We are attracted to literature produced by people with a more liberal practice than ourselves, often people we would not associate closely with in real life. We seem to have a confused mindset that equates greater liberality with greater spiritual enlightenment. Most of us would not look to, say, the Amish for spiritual help. But we are quick to devour mainstream Protestant books. We appear to betray a secret belief that liberals, of both theology and practice, are spiritually liberated and have something to teach us. If we really believe this, we will follow a few steps behind them and one day be where they are.

Be cautious with "Christian" books. If you picked up a book on Islam, your spiritual guard would be on high alert. When you read a book with a Christian label that quotes from the Bible and sounds good, you are in a vulnerable position. This includes books on godly womanhood, dating, marriage, and sexual purity. If you read books like this, don't read alone. Get your parents' opinion or find a trusted older woman who enjoys reading to review it for you. Be open about your reading material with the ladies at your church. Ask what they're reading and share what you're reading. It can be a fun conversation starter and give you more reading ideas, but more than that, it builds a sense of accountability and openness. We tend to think these little areas of our lives don't matter, but we could benefit from a stronger sense of accountability in the private areas of our lives.

We may connect with a woman's writing and feel like we are getting answers, but who are these women? How do they practice their faith? Being female does not give them more validity than our male pastors. If we need help from a woman in a specific area, it would be safer and more beneficial to share with mature women we know and get help in the context of relationship and accountability.

What about reading for entertainment? Reading for fun is a broad-ranging subject and what is considered appropriate varies in different homes. Honor the wishes of your parents. Borrow books from trusted people and seek good book recommendations from people who like to read. Memorize the names of good authors so you can recognize them.

Old classics are generally good. Beware of new popular books that are called classic—that's not the same thing. Often, memoirs are good, depending on what part of their lives the authors focus on and whether they include profanity and immorality. Biographies and autobiographies of godly people or important historical figures are usually good choices. It's fiction that often gets young women in trouble because of romantic or sexual appeal and the fantasy it may fuel.

Be honest with yourself. If you want to read a mostly-okay book for a scene or two that feeds something lustful in you, be wise and don't do it. Sometimes you may start reading something, unaware of what is in it. If you find it isn't good for you, put it down. Get it away from where it will tempt you. It can be tough to stop reading in the middle of the story, but scenes from books have a way of burning themselves into our minds. It's not worth dealing with years of unwanted memory pop-ups just because we couldn't say no to our curiosity.

You know your weaknesses in this area. Don't go to the library alone if that's a temptation for you. Reading on a device is private and can be a source of temptation. Be accountable to someone. Just don't do it if you can't handle it. Jesus said that if your hand causes you to sin, it is better to cut it off than to go to hell (Matthew 5:30). This sounds dramatic, but he made a point about taking serious action to avoid sinning. Canceling your Kindle subscription could be what cutting off your hand means for you.

MUSIC

What is on your most-listened-to music lists on your

streaming service? Or what music CDs do you have in your possession? Would you be happy to show anyone who asked to see it?

You might argue that your listening habits don't matter. Music may seem purely recreational, but we can't deny its powerful attraction to our souls. The type of music you are attracted to reflects your inner peace or lack of peace. What sound speaks to your depths: beautiful harmonies or chaotic dissonance? Consider your music against this checklist.

- Does your music stir your mind to worship with meaningful lyrics and beautiful harmonies, or does it make you feel melancholy and restless?
- Do you feel like you want to be a better person after listening to it, or do you only feel good while listening to it and irritable afterward?
- Do you want to sing along and find yourself singing later, or is your music difficult to sing because of its composition or simply isn't fit to sing in front of anyone?
- If it's instrumental, does it make the girl inside feel peaceful and lovely or incite the beast of self-will and rebellion?

Sometimes young people experiment with listening to cultural music offerings against their parents' and church's wishes. What do they think an immoral cultural idol has to offer them? The lyrics of many pop songs glorify uncontrolled emotional and sexual behavior. You cannot listen to music that promotes impure behavior and have a pure heart and mind!

Humans tend to believe that they can compartmentalize their lives: *I can do this in private, and it won't affect the rest of my life.* What happens in secret, inside you, will eventually come through. You cannot be impure on the inside and pure on the outside; you cannot be both a bottom feeder and an angelfish.

Music can be a much-argued topic, and I am not here to give you specific direction—your parents and churches can do that. But you know better than anyone else what you're listening to and why you're listening to it. Music should not be a crutch that we must have to survive emotionally. Do you have to hide your music habits? You may feel justified in this because your church's or parents' music standards don't permit something that you think is okay or because "everyone else is doing it." At this point, the okay-ness of the music becomes irrelevant—the secrecy and rebellion are the problem. No matter how "okay" the music may be, what matters is whether you live in obedience and openness. Your authorities do not make silly and unnecessary rules just because they can. They have reasons for their boundaries.

ONLINE INFLUENCE

In this digital age, we also need to consider the impact of internet influencers, such as bloggers, YouTubers, and podcast hosts. We must recognize that a charismatic personality with the ability to gain a following may not have anything of substance to offer us. Having a platform does not equal credibility. In other words, a person's ability to create YouTube, blog, or podcast content and gather followers does not automatically make them an authority on anything.

It is very unwise to embrace something promoted by an internet influencer over the teaching of your home ministry. Unlike your pastor, such a person operates alone, without the structure and accountability of a church to give validity to his or her message. Influencers can comfortably project their ideas into cyberspace while taking no responsibility for the fallout of the ideas they promote. For example, a blogger's dating practices should not carry more weight with you and your boyfriend than what your parents or pastor want for you. If someone online whom you do not know says you can kiss, it sounds more appealing than the strict standard your parents or pastor would like for you. But why would you take his word for it? That person will likely never know you exist. He will probably never speak face-to-face with you, lie awake at night worrying over you, take time out to try to help you in person, or be there to help you pick up the pieces if you fail. Your parents and your ministry care about your life and want the best for you. They are the people who are there when you need them.

I encourage you to consider how and where you are receiving spiritual nourishment. What you feed the girl inside determines her loveliness. Above all, do not discount the relevance of God's Word and the sincerity of Christian mentors around you.

Chapter Eleven

Your Mother

A young woman's most valuable resource for navigating life is a good relationship with her mother. Your mother has more life experience than you and knows you quite well. It would seem that mothers and daughters should naturally coexist harmoniously: they are both females, they share genetics, they live together. But the very things that ought to bond them can sometimes come between them. Why is this?

A teenage daughter was once a darling little pig-tailed girl who sat on her mother's lap to hear stories read aloud. She carried fistfuls of wilted wildflowers to Mom and came to her for Band-Aids. She pulled up a kitchen chair to help bake cookies. Her mother thought she was cute and sweet, and the little girl thought her mother was the best person in the universe.

Why should misunderstandings, tension, possibly even stony silences and harsh accusations ever need to enter this picture?

It doesn't need to, but sometimes it does. Not all teenagers have trouble relating to their mothers. But if you do, let's consider what might be going on.

WHAT HAPPENS?

Somewhere between the storybooks and Band-Aids of childhood and the transition to womanhood, the relationship sometimes breaks down. Girls tend to blame this on their mothers—after all, they are the grownups; they're supposed to know what they're doing. Instead of placing all the blame and responsibility on your mother, ask yourself what you could change to improve the situation. You are the only one who can change the relationship from your side of things.

Young women tend to be super hard on their mothers. They may hold them to a strict standard and be reluctant to forgive them for not being perfect. They may think their mothers are old-fashioned and don't understand modern times. It could be true that a mother doesn't completely understand everything. Times do change, and pressures evolve. However, your mother was a young woman once, and many basic things about what it's like to be young don't change. She probably understands far more than you think she does, and that's why she has rules and cautions that don't make sense to you.

You used to think your mother was one of the most wonderful people in the world. Remember the six-year-old I-love-you scrawls drawn with wobbly hearts? Now you are crying into your bedspread because she won't let you go to the party or make your dress the way "everybody" else does. Or perhaps she scolded you for your bad attitude, and you feel she doesn't understand you. It's a mystery how this happens because mothers love their daughters, and most don't intentionally try to make their children's lives difficult. Your mother might not have much of an idea of how to be a good mom, but maybe you haven't had much practice being a good daughter either.

Lack of communication can be a problem: the two of you spend so much time together that you can assume a lot of things are understood when they aren't. Both of you may imagine insults and insinuations where none were intended. Both of you may feel unloved by a misunderstood word or gesture. Possibly she gave you a gift she thought you'd like, and you feel unloved and misunderstood because she doesn't even know what you want. The unhappy vibes you send her may make her feel unloved and misunderstood because she tried so hard, but it didn't work. It could be she has a habit of talking to her friends about you, which she does not mean unkindly but which you find ultra-embarrassing—after all, you're not a two-year-old anymore!

Kind honesty is probably the best way to clear up these misunderstandings and miscommunications. It's best not to pretend you are okay when you aren't, or excited about things you don't like. You'll be left feeling resentful, and she might buy you another one like it, which gets awfully complicated. It's never okay to be ugly in your communication, but it might be better to admit you're not fond of the shoes right away, while they can be returned if she gives you that option. Don't make a big deal out of everything, though. You wouldn't have picked the sky-blue fabric with daisies—it's so last century—but she thinks it looks nice on you, and it won't kill you to wear it now and then.

If it really bothers you when she tells stories about you to her friends, you could calmly and kindly tell her you find it embarrassing. However, you probably shouldn't be quite so offended by it. It's likely not as demeaning as you think. Maybe in some roundabout way, she thinks she's bragging on you. Instead of being angry with her for not understanding you, spend some time trying to understand her. What is she really feeling? What is she not saying? Be mature on your side of the relationship.

If your mother feels controlling and constantly offers unsolicited advice, you may feel offended, which in turn offends her. *Of course I'll behave tonight—do you think I'm planning to get into trouble? Of course I'll try to drive safely—I don't want to be in an accident either! Yes, I remember my curfew; I don't have Alzheimer's yet.* Don't take it all so personally. Even if she doesn't go about it in the best way, it indicates her love and concern for you. If she did not care about you, she would ignore you. You could be out all night, and she wouldn't ask where you'd been. That would be far worse than anything you're dealing with.

Maybe you know in your heart that your mom loves you, but she has never told you so. She might not be one for hugging or words of affirmation, and you wish she would be. She may not have learned to express herself well. Perhaps she feels insecure herself. Maybe you two have different love languages and what she offers is not what would mean the most to you.

Aside from problems such as unexpressed love and good-but-misguided-intentions, you may feel like you carry legitimate hurts from the relationship. She may have hurt you emotionally in her anger and frustration. Don't turn your wounds and scars into impenetrable armor that permanently estranges you from your mother and home. Learn to forgive from Jesus' example. You are not more special than he was, and he forgave horrible behavior.

Learn how to say "I'm sorry." You might feel like your mother owes you apologies. Show her how it's done. Don't overbuild idealistic expectations for your relationship. She's not perfect, and neither are you. Both of you will keep on making mistakes. Learn how to apologize when it's you and how to forgive when it's her. You can grow up and move away from your mother, but if you marry and have your own family, you will find yourself again enmeshed in close family relationships. If you don't learn different patterns of relating, you will find yourself using the same ones with your own family. Vowing to have a different home life is not enough. You must forgive and reconcile with your mother and home before you are whole enough to live differently.

THINGS TO CONSIDER

Your mother may face stresses you don't know about that have nothing to do with you. She may be in disagreement with your father, worried about a wayward sibling, concerned about church problems, or even stressed about issues with her own parents or siblings. You could be an unsuspecting scapegoat when you do something foolish or catch her at a low moment. Her problems do not give her the right to mistreat you, but she's only human. Give her the benefit of the doubt, and don't take it too personally.

She may be experiencing hormonal upheaval. Teenage girls do not have a monopoly on hormones. Studies show that women who live together tend to cycle together. This means you may both experience PMS at the same time. This doesn't excuse either of you, but it could explain why it seems you both got out of bed on the wrong side on the same day. She may have been as surprised and upset by her irritated response as you were. Give each other some space and grace.

She may have never learned to relate well to her own mother, and she struggles to know how to relate to you. She may think her relationship with you is a big improvement over what she had. Accept and appreciate her efforts, no matter how inadequate they seem to you. She may feel intimidated by you. Teenage girls can be very self-confident, talented, and intimidating people.

Maybe you have an idealized relationship in your mind that will not happen. You didn't pick your mother; she didn't pick you. God put you together. You both have to work with what you get. His grace working in both of your hearts can accomplish amazing things. You may never have the type of relationship you'd like to, but that doesn't mean you can't improve what you have.

Focus on all the things you can be thankful for in your relationship with your mother. You may think there aren't very many, but remember that you are close to the situation, and your feelings are involved. Realize also that you're probably being idealistic and perhaps a little unfair. Create a list of everything your mother does for you and everything you like about her. This simple shift of thought could make a big difference for you. Insisting on clinging to her faults and your real or imagined wounds is unforgiveness and will stunt your progress in life.

If you do have a good relationship with your mother, treasure it. Let her know you appreciate her. There is probably nothing else that will be a more significant help and comfort to you as you find your way through the maze of growing up. Your relationship with your mother is one of your first and most extended. You can't ever really escape it.

If you do not get along well with your mother, trying to escape from and ignore her is not a solution. You will want her at your wedding. She'll be the grandmother of any children you have. Very likely, there will come a day in the not-so-distant future when you'll want to call her for advice on something, even if it's just a recipe. Your mother will always be your mother as long as both of you are alive. A mother is not like a best friend who turned out to not be a good friend after all or an ex-boyfriend you decided to remove from your life. You cannot dump her. Therefore, your best option is to make peace in your heart with the mother you have, *just the way she is.*

MENTORS

If you find it challenging to share with your mother, you may be drawn to another woman with whom you find it easier to talk. There is nothing wrong with this, even if you have a good relationship with your mother, but in doing so, be careful not to reject your mother. She birthed you and cared for you. She probably loves you more than anyone else in the world, even if you have difficulty feeling it. She is probably proud of you, even if she never says so. She has much more invested in you than a woman you just got close to recently. She will always be your mom, through bad times and good, reunions and distances, shared memories and griefs. She deserves your love and respect and continued effort to improve the relationship.

A good mentor will not try to usurp your mother but will encourage you in your efforts to repair the relationship. While allowing for honest conversation, both of you should speak respectfully of your mother and your home. It is unhealthy for you to become involved with someone who speaks negatively of your home or your mother. Christians should put away bitterness, anger, and evil speaking and forgive as Christ has forgiven (Ephesians 4:31). Counselling can fuel evil speaking if the mentor or counselor encourages you to complain about people.

Sharing how you have been wronged may seem right and helpful because it feels good. It can build an intense but fragile bond between you and your mentor as you revel in feeling understood. But it will not provide the true security and love you crave, and it will not bring you closer to your mother. Choose a mentor who will assist you in repairing relationships, not deepening divides. Love your mother and do all you can to have a good relationship with her.

Remember that how you relate to your mother is likely how your children will relate to you. Be the daughter you'd want to have. Make things right where needed. Take the initiative to make good memories together. If your mother passed away suddenly, you would have to live with regrets about what you should have done. No mother is perfect, but every mother is special. You only have one mother. Do something nice for her today.

Chapter Twelve

Your Home

Your home is full of relationships—and, hopefully, some of your favorite people. Home is the place you return to at the end of a day, the space in which you coexist with family members in harmony and sometimes a little chaos. Maybe you drive each other crazy on occasion, but you miss each other like crazy when apart. The home you grow up in is typically a special place of belonging and acceptance. A family develops routines and practices that become a unique element of what we call home. You may recall staying overnight at a friend's house as a child and being surprised and unsettled by how different things were there. Things were *right* at your house.

As you grow older, you might not think things are so perfect at your house anymore. You see your parents' flaws and mistakes. You might be tempted to be critical of your parents. After all, if you live in a Christian home, shouldn't it be perfect—or the next thing to it? While some so-called Christian homes do have inexcusable problems, most are not-so-bad, just not-perfect homes. Don't disown and distance yourself from your home and family; they are part of you.

Your home is likely happier than you think it is. If your parents took you to church every Sunday, you are part of just 22% of fortunate church-going children in America.[1] If you've always had enough to eat, you are better off than 10.7 million children—or one in seven children—in the United States who do not always have enough food and may even be starving.[2] If you have never seen either of your parents under the influence of drugs or alcohol, you are more fortunate than one in eight—or 8.7 million—American children.[3] If you have a mom and a dad in your home who are in their first marriage, you are part of only 50% of your peers who are so blessed.[4] The other half have experienced the pain of fractured home life. Things are no longer right at their houses.

GOOD, BUT NOT PERFECT

Part of the reason Christian young people may struggle to appreciate their parents is because they are intensely idealistic; they want to be perfect; they want life to be perfect. Strangely enough, young people can project their longings for perfection onto everyone else while completely missing their own glaring faults.

Parents are far from perfect, and they know it. Parenting is not as simple as it looks like it ought to be. When parents reach the age where they have teenagers, they may feel like they know very little about anything, and the task of parenting may look gargantuan. Their own youthful idealism has likely melted away in the face of realities and disappointments over the years.

Parents sometimes tend to hide their insecurity and bluff their way through, which can cause resentment. A young person may think *You act like you know everything, but you're making a colossal mess of things.* This can fuel resentment and drive wedges into relationships. If both of you can be open about mistakes, things will improve. Understand that whether or not your parents admit to failures or uncertainties, they probably feel them and are not as confident as they appear. Accept this and give them some grace, just as you wish for grace from them sometimes: when you've dented the family vehicle, burned the food, or completely forgot the errand they asked you to do. We all need grace sometimes.

Anger, frustration, and depression in parents can create deep resentment in their children. Youth may look on contemptuously as they witness their parents struggling—and sometimes losing—in these areas. *So, you're a mature Christian, and you act like that, huh? How can I ever respect you?* While parents may struggle with many things their children are unaware of, there is no justification for sinful behavior. However, your parents' failings do not justify bad behavior on your part. We are all sinners saved by grace, and we all need to account for our own lives, regardless of what others have done or not done to us.

Parents can hurt and neglect their children, sometimes in large, but often in small, ways. A sensitive child can internalize many unintentional hurts. Emotional pain can be as real as physical pain. The key to healing these wounds is acknowledging hurts and deliberately forgiving your parents. Emotional pain and insecurity are a result of the fall and human imperfection. Both of you are broken in ways you do not even realize. Our humanity will cause problems in relationships all our lives. Jesus helps us forbear and forgive and love anyway.

Don't wait for your parents to ask for your forgiveness before you forgive them. They may be unaware of the list of faults you hold against them. They don't even need to know about it for you to make peace with them. It's probably not necessary for you to dredge up all the hurts and let them know how badly they've hurt you. There may be a place for this in some situations, but making them feel pain too is not necessary for you to forgive: Christ's blood covers all that.

How can you improve a difficult relationship with your parents?

- Acknowledge that you've been hurt. You might even make a list—but then tear it up and throw it away.
- Believe that your parents have tried to do their best for you even if it seems like they didn't.
- Believe that they love you and have always loved you, even when they didn't know how to show it.
- Forgive them. Let the past go; it doesn't need to rule your life today.
- Take steps to restore the relationship if necessary, even if they are tiny steps.

Forgiveness doesn't mean you condone wrong behavior. It doesn't mean you weren't hurt. It doesn't mean you will never think about the hurts again or that the forgiveness will be automatic or immediately complete. Forgiveness simply means laying down your feelings of resentment and anger—every time they come back. That's it. *It's true, but I'm going to let it go.*

There is a quasi-satisfying feeling of vengeance in nurturing unforgiveness. We feel like we somehow get even with someone when we refuse to forgive them. But holding a grudge doesn't hurt the other person all that much; it hurts us far more. We can waste a lot of time and energy on negative thinking and hinder our spiritual progress. Being consumed with negative emotions can even ruin your physical health. Releasing those feelings in forgiveness frees us and feels far better than nurturing them.

RELATIONSHIP WITH PARENTS

The Bible offers clear direction for parent-child relationships. "Children, obey your parents in the Lord [that is, accept their guidance and discipline as His representatives], for this is right [for obedience teaches wisdom and self-discipline]. Honor [esteem, value as precious] your father and your mother [and be respectful to them]—this is the first commandment with a promise—so that it may be well with you, and that you may have a long life on the earth" (Ephesians 6:1-3 AMP). As long as you are living in your parent's home and they are responsible for you, this applies to you; even after you've left their home, the honor and respect last for a lifetime. This command does not have exceptions, such as "you only have to do this if you like the way they do things," or "you only have to obey them if they're perfect."

Young people sometimes accuse their parents of not being there for them, not answering their questions, or knowing what they need. Always waiting for others is an immature approach to life. We cannot expect others always to notice our needs and offer us exactly what we need. We need to learn how to make our needs known. Let your parents know what questions you have or ask for their advice.

Try to break unhealthy cycles in the way you relate. Don't bring home a piece of clothing and make a scene, hoping they'll give in and let you wear it; instead, ask their advice on what to wear. Choose to honor what you already know to be their preference. Much of the tension between parents and daughters arises from daughters pushing the line of what they know to be acceptable, constantly trying to nudge the line out a little farther. If you make choices you know your parents would approve of, you will not need to deal with tension caused by rebellion. If you're being rebellious, you can't fairly blame the strain on your parents or label them cranky and old-fashioned.

Don't relate to them in fight-mode: instead of going to them with three arguments for why you ought to be allowed to go somewhere, be prepared to accept the fact that they may think you've been going away too much, and a night at home with the family would be beneficial. Chances are that if you sweetly stay home and play games with the family, they will view you as more mature and thus be more willing to let you go next time. Of course, staying home with a poor attitude won't have the same effect.

Sometimes you may think your parents are trying to hold you back and not allow you to grow up. It could be that you are not as mature as you imagine. It is also possible that sometimes parents don't realize that their children are maturing and continue to treat them like small children. You can't go inside their heads and adjust their thinking, but you can control your response. Don't yell and slam doors and be the child they seem to think you are. Be calm and civilized. Show them some respect, and they'll probably show you some.

RELATIONSHIP WITH SIBLINGS

Likely you get along with some of your siblings better than others. This is normal. Your placement in the family may have something to do with it; siblings close in age sometimes feel a need to compete with each other as they may subconsciously feel there is not enough space in the family for both. Personalities also affect how we get along—those with different personalities often coexist better than those with similar personalities, particularly if both are more outgoing.

You may make a less secure sibling feel insecure and jealous if you are confident, aggressive, and talented. You could run over them and make them feel inferior while barely noticing what you're doing. They may be more sensitive than you and take your comments far more personally than you intend. Rather than putting yourself in the limelight, taking charge, and doing all the talking, encourage them to participate, try to draw them out, and wait for them to speak.

Maybe you are the insecure one. Your talented sister always seems to say and do the right things and gracefully waltz through life while you're stumbling, stammering, and uncertain. Siblings can grow up with resentment that can last a lifetime if not resolved, but it doesn't have to be that way. Rather than being resentful, realize you are no less valuable than any of your siblings. You are equal in God's eyes. You have your own talents and your own space to fill, both in your home and in God's kingdom.

Even if you can't place the source of conflict, try to get along. It is not okay for a Christian to misbehave at home with people who are "only family." The Golden Rule—do unto others as you would have them do unto you—certainly applies to siblings just as much as everyone else (Matthew 7:12).

This is often an area of struggle for young Christians—they want to get along more peaceably with siblings, but their carnal feelings flare up as they always did; only now they feel guiltier because they're supposed to be Christians. Becoming a Christian doesn't automatically fix these things. You will have to make an effort. Look for the good in your siblings. Disarm them with unexpected kindness. Avoid potential disagreements with an unexpected response, such as, “sure, you can mow the yard, and I’ll clean bathrooms,” even though you prefer mowing. Apologize rather than defend: “I’m sorry. I was rude.” Look for things you have in common or go out of your way to show interest in their interests.

The root of relational struggles is selfishness. Being unselfish is not easy. It is something you will work on your whole life. Family life offers personal relationship practice that will be valuable to you later. Don’t think you will grow up and get away from this sort of thing. There will always be difficult relationships to navigate, and they don’t necessarily get easier.

HAPPILY-EVER-AFTER SYNDROME

Sometimes youth are frustrated with their homes because they don’t think they are good enough. Because their parents are not perfect, they may question whether they’re good Christians. Conservative Christian teaching indoctrinates us with idealistic preaching and teaching that urges us to grow spiritually and strive for perfection. We read stories and books that end ideally: the appropriate apologies are offered, the bad guys are punished with car accidents or broken legs—or if they’re little children, a spanking—justice is meted out so that the righteous are saved from disasters or rewarded with ice cream sundaes. No one in a “Christian” story would raise their voice in frustration; if they did, they’d apologize. We close these books and re-enter real life where we see everyone’s failings, failings people don’t always apologize for, and even if they do, they may repeat. It may look like sin goes unpunished and right choices go unnoticed.

The idealism intended to encourage us may seem confusing

and frustrating. We may feel like our parents aren't good enough because they're not perfect. Nothing and no one is ideal on earth. Jesus' teaching urges us to a perfection that is not easy to attain. The Sermon on the Mount is full of behavior that we are to strive for but which does not come naturally to us.

The Bible gives us many candid accounts of the failings of saints. God knows we are human and forgives us for being human. Jesus calls Christians to follow his example and forgive each other. The failures of godly people do not mean we all should give up because we can't be perfect.

Whether you feel your home life is normal or should be improved, always seek to grow in your relationships with your parents and siblings. Don't create distance. Moving away from home because you can't get along with someone should only be done with the motive of restoring the relationship. Trying to get away from your home is not good if you are not actively trying to resolve relationship struggles. You can leave Mom and Dad and their methods of relating behind, but you take yourself and your methods along. You can't escape the fact that you are a product of your home, and it is best to solve your problems at their root. Some relationships are impossible to reconcile in the way we would like, but even small steps to repair them can be healing.

If you feel like your home has severe problems and want to share your struggles with someone and get help, seek guidance from people who already know you and your family. Be willing to accept input from those who are close to your situation. Human nature often prefers help from people far away or uninvolved who will focus on our point of view. But your best mentors are likely adults who are already in your life.

Focus on the blessings of your home life. They are likely far more significant than you think. A home does not need to be perfect to be a place of warmth, security, love, and acceptance. Treasure your home, and fill your place in it with joy. Try to live in such a way that you do not have a lot of regrets.

Chapter Thirteen

Your Girlfriends

Girlfriend relationships are important. Being with friends is not only fun, but it's also profoundly satisfying. Girls take many pictures with their friends: drinking coffee, eating out, and shopping. Girls smile a lot in these pictures.

Time spent with a friend is much more than sharing good coffee, gourmet food, and fun experiences. Interaction with friends plays a vital role in your life and is necessary for good emotional health. I like to see a young woman with friends, especially one with many friends, not just a select few. Your youth is a good time of life to develop deep and lasting connections that are much more beneficial than wasting time crushing on and chasing after boys. If you struggle to relate to young men appropriately, my advice is to direct your attention to developing more meaningful relationships with young women. Many times, boy-crazy young women are the lonely ones who lack close girl friendships.

MORE THAN ROMANCE

I am happily married. When my children asked me recently to name my two best friends, I asked, "You mean two besides your dad? Or the person who comes next after him?" I found out later that they asked him the same thing, and he said, "You mean besides your mom?" I consider him my closest friend, and I love spending time with him; however, I still enjoy being with women. Friendships with women fill a different part of me; this is healthy.

Women tend to long for and pursue romance in order to fill longings that it cannot fill. Our culture is so romantically saturated that we all probably do this a little; women expect a lot from romance. We get the impression that romance is better and more important than friendship. I once heard someone challenge the trend of calling spouses best friends because it ties intimacy and friendship too closely together in a culture that sexualizes everything. They pointed out that this concept leaves singles out in the cold: since they don't have romance, they are left with "just" friends. Whether or not that is a bad idea, I do believe that romance can be so overrated that friendship becomes underrated by default.

You may have to be married a little while to find it out, but your life will be more meaningful if you embrace the value of women friendships. Women friends just "get" each other—especially friends you've known for years, but sometimes new ones surprise you too. You can enjoy long-distance relationships from your past, even if you don't hear from each other often. You can make new friends and discover new things in common as life brings you in contact with new people. One of the beauties of girlfriends is the natural space in the relationship. Unless you are single and rooming together, you don't usually live together. You don't have to work through all the nitty-gritty of who misplaced the checkbook, forgot the appointment, hung the toilet paper roll backward—or didn't replace it—or who ought to get up with the crying child. These annoyances, when dealt with properly, are what ultimately make a marriage deep, close and meaningful in a different way than another relationship, but it's refreshing to enjoy relationships without this element.

If you begin dating, don't drop your girlfriends like hot potatoes. Your romance is not a replacement, a fill-all, be-all, end-all thing; it's something extra, something different. Besides, your friends don't deserve that. Your relationships with your closest friends will go through an adjustment period as you turn more time and energy toward your boyfriend; you will naturally share more with him and less with them as the relationship progresses. This is perfectly normal. But don't leave your best friend completely out in the cold. Be considerate of the needs she still has for companionship, even though you may not feel the same. And don't just spend time with her to patronize her. You still need her too, even if you don't feel it now. If you were to break up, you would need her. And someday, when you realize romance is not everything, you'll be glad to spend time with her.

The same goes for relocating, whether you or your friend has moved. Marriage often parts friends. Keeping in touch with old friends helps to ease the transition into new friendships. There is nothing like meeting up with an old friend with whom you share a lot of history and picking up where you left off. These are bonds to treasure.

Continue to make friends and nurture relationships with women as an adult. We can place unfair burdens on our husbands by expecting an exclusive relationship with them to meet all our needs. They can feel pressured, resentful and inadequate for they know not what. A woman can turn to her husband, expecting the fulfillment she got from her mom, three sisters, and five girlfriends. It's simply not possible. Spending time with other women cheers and energizes us, making both us and our husbands happier.

Incorporate both your husband's friends and your own into your relationship as you date and get married. My husband and I were the first among our closest friends to marry, so they were single when we were newlyweds. Sometimes we invited our friends in turn to our home, enjoying supper together; then one of us would go read a book or something while giving the other time with friends. It was fun, and our friends loved it.

An interesting development in female relationships is that as you marry and have children or move on in other ways, you will likely grow closer to your mom and sisters. Relating to your family when all of you are grownups brings a special dimension to your relationship. Even if your paths separate widely from your sisters, there is always a special bond between people who grew up in the same home. Value it and treat your sisters as special friends. Keep in touch in small ways. Remember birthdays. Call or message each other. Be interested in each other's lives, even if hundreds of miles separate you.

FRIENDSHIP EVALUATION

Use your time as a single woman to make deep friendships with young women who are spiritually encouraging to you, women you will be able to reconnect with later in life, women who will be there for you when you need them. Consider who your closest friends are. What do they do for you?

- Do your closest friends inspire you to be a better Christian? Or do they make you question what you believe?
- Do you feel good about the time you spend with them and part ways refreshed? Or do you live unhappily for the next time you'll be together?
- Does your family like and accept your friends? Are your friends comfortable in your home? Or do you prefer to spend your time together away from your home?
- Do your friends help you respect your church, ministry, and parents? Or do they make you feel unsettled and rebellious?
- Would you be proud to have your closest friends in your bridal party if you got married? I've heard it said that you should choose people for your wedding party who will encourage you to be faithful to your marriage.

Consider these questions in reverse as well. What are you doing for your friends? Are you dragging them down with negativity, gossip, or criticism of others? Are you inspiring them to be better Christians? Can they count on you when they need someone? Do you faithfully keep their secrets, not only the personal things they share but the things you know about them because you are close to them?

CLIQUES AND BEST FRIENDS

Is it okay to have a best friend or a small group of best friends? What constitutes a clique? It is normal, even healthy, to be closer to some friends than others. It is impossible to be best friends with everyone. But you've probably heard caution against cliques. A clique is "a small group of people with shared interests or other features in common who spend time together and do not readily allow others to join them." The problem with cliques is not that we have best friends; the problem is the exclusivity.

When I was nineteen, I attended a youth Bible school for six weeks with two of my best friends. Toward the end of our time there, the matron complimented us on our behavior. It had taken her a long time to figure out we were a best friend trio from the same youth group. I had not consciously thought about avoiding cliquishness, but all of us had been interested in making new friends. I do not relate this to brag but to show that if you are secure in your friendships and open to new friendships, this problem will probably take care of itself.

Don't pour all your energy into one or two relationships. Improve your ability to make new friends and enjoy the diversity of new relationships along with the old ones. Your best friend is the one you'd always turn to in a crisis; keep that knowledge in your pocket as a kind of security and enjoy time with others. Save your best friend heart-to-heart for when you are alone. When with a group, stay with the group and make everyone feel included. There is a time and a place for one-on-one sharing, but it's not in a group setting. Don't run away from the group or get quiet when others join you.

What if you feel your best friend is drifting away from you, or you sense that she is making a new best friend? Or maybe someone you'd like to be best friends with doesn't seem to feel the same way about you. The funny thing about close friendships is that you cannot force them; they either happen or don't happen. If you feel a close friend is moving away from you, let her go. You can't force her to be your best friend. It might be worth considering what kind of relationship you had with her.

Maybe she wasn't a good influence on you. Perhaps the relationship was too exclusive, and she felt smothered. Maybe it was nothing you did or didn't do, and you just grew apart from each other. Either way, do not allow it to crush you and make you feel inferior. If you haven't been cliquish, you already have a network of other friends to be with, and you will probably make a new best friend.

Do not ignore girls who are difficult to relate to. As Christians, we're expected to love our enemies (Matthew 5:44) and treat others how we'd like to be treated (Matthew 7:12). Jesus wants you to reach out to girls who seem to be social misfits. It's much easier to worry about what the popular girls will think if you befriend that left-out person than how that outcast girl feels—being friendly when you don't feel like it is not easy. Doing your part in behaving wisely and maturely and including everyone will bless you and others.

APPROPRIATE BOUNDARIES

There are appropriate boundaries and behaviors surrounding girl-to-girl relationships, just as there are for girl-boy relationships. While it is appropriate for girls to share bathrooms and sleeping and dressing areas, girls among girls need a level of modesty and privacy. Sometimes we emphasize modesty around boys to the extent that it may seem modesty is only for when boys are around. This is not true. We need a basic level of physical reserve with any human to whom we are not married. Nakedness is never appropriate. This applies to swimwear as well. If you wouldn't wear it at a slumber party, why is poolside any different?

Touch is often important to girls. Hugs, pats, and shoulder massages are great; we all thrive on appropriate human contact.

But there are also boundaries here. Girls should not cuddle in ways that are appropriate only for married people. Constantly needing to touch and hang on to one another indicates neediness and insecurity.

What if you have a thought or a feeling about a girlfriend that causes you to wonder if you are experiencing something lesbian—that is, "romantically attracted to other women"? First, just because you had the thought or feeling does not mean you are of a lesbian orientation. Our culture promotes sexual experimentation and deviation: people seem to be proud of being anything but heterosexual, and confuse themselves by fixating on confusion. Don't be unduly alarmed or ashamed by such thoughts. Inappropriate thoughts or feelings toward the same gender are not more sinful than wrong thoughts or feelings toward the opposite gender. They may be less common, but both are sinful thoughts to be discarded and not dwelt upon.

If lesbian thoughts are a big problem for you or you have acted on your thoughts, confess this to someone and seek counsel and accountability to live in victory. The key difference between a Christian's sexual urges and the sexual desires of non-Christians is self-expression; our culture says that if you feel it, you should act on it. Our culture has capitalized on homosexuality as trendy and notice-worthy. People are lauded for "coming out" and telling the world their sexual orientation as though they have done something courageous when it is, in fact, submitting to being controlled by sin. The Bible says clearly that all sexual urges outside of marriage—marriage between one man and one woman—should be controlled, that we should think pure thoughts, and that we should subdue our fleshly instincts.

The church has often overreacted to homosexuality, placing it in a deep, dark category of its own. While homosexual temptation is obviously different than heterosexual temptation, *it is not more sinful*. It is not a special case of humiliation. It is a struggle with sin comparable to other sins.

If you struggle with lesbian thoughts and desires, focus on right and pure thoughts. Avoid behavior and situations that bring temptation. Connect with women in meaningful and healthy ways. Think about how you can give in your relationships rather than being a taker.

Beware of unhealthy emotional attachments, possessiveness, and a desire to control others. If you feel a compulsion to be with one friend, constantly message her, and know what she's doing at all times, your relationship is in an unhealthy place. Likely you are looking to that relationship to fill something for you that it cannot. Our longings for emotional attachment have legitimate fulfillment in a relationship with God and healthy relationships with others. Focus first of all on your relationship with God. Then think about what you have to offer to the people closest to you.

Chapter Fourteen

The Search

There are supposedly around eight thousand dating sites in the world. That's a lot of people looking for love! Like women everywhere who seek the perfect romantic partner, conservative young women are on the ultimate high alert for perfect young men. Of course, when you believe God intends marriage to be a lifetime commitment, making a wise choice is essential. But sometimes, the biblical directive to marry "only in the Lord" (1 Corinthians 7:39) doesn't seem like enough of a standard. We'd like to find a super-giant Christian young man.

We tend to hear a lot of teaching directed to young men, inspiring them to higher ideals of godly manhood; this is good. Parents, especially fathers, tend to be more involved in their daughter's romantic relationships than in past years; this is positive. Young women tend to hear much more about what to look for in a young man; this could be problematic, since they may take it a little too far sometimes.

Some of the extra teaching and precautions we hear come as a positive reaction to failed marriages of the past. There have been naïve women who married men who were a huge disappointment to them: dishonest, unfaithful, perhaps abusive. No one wants that to happen. But we may have gotten a little bit too picky. It's not a sin to say no to a young man who asks you out. It's not wrong to break up with him if you're uncomfortable with the relationship. The danger is over-correcting into looking for men so perfect they don't even exist. We can quickly place the bar too high for any human being to reach. Women can also put men under a microscope and never let them out, even after marriage. This treatment is not fair. When we raise our standards too high, we appear to expect the majority of Christian young men to be losers; this is not true.

IDEALS FOR A POTENTIAL HUSBAND

There is a popular assignment in youth Bible classes that young women can get carried away with: to list ideals for your future spouse. While it is a good exercise, it applies only to a few main principles. It is not permission to make a fantasy concrete. Such a list should not be personalized, specifying hair color or preferred hobbies, for example, or blatantly self-centered: *I want him to enjoy the things I enjoy*. I don't think we should wish for a specific temperament—isn't that discounting surprises God may have in store for us? We don't often do well at knowing what we want or need in any area of life. The more specific you get about what you want, the more you may fuel a fantasy figure in your mind of a superhuman man you're not going to find.

God does not give anyone a perfect spouse who always does everything right and consistently keeps them happy. He gives us imperfect people, like ourselves. Someone has suggested that we will probably get eighty percent of what we really want from our spouses. If we went looking for a better person, we'd get about eighty percent from him too. Maybe you observe married couples you know and imagine they found near-perfection in each other. In reality, marriage is an intense relationship that takes work, no matter who you marry. You don't see what goes on behind the scenes.

Maybe adults should just make a list for young women. Something like:

- Respects his parents
- Treats his mother well
- Isn't lazy
- Supports his church
- Honest
- Polite

Perhaps even with a disclaimer: *these qualities in moderation, with allowance for growth.* Any man has a chance at living up to these things, even an un-cool guy, a not-good-looking one, one with a speech impediment, one who has never traveled out of the country, or one who blushes a lot. Any good-hearted young man deserves respect and a chance to become something more than what he is now. No one has the right to question his sincerity automatically unless there is proof.

When a young man asks you for a date, be a true lady and take it as a compliment, no matter who he is. I'm not sure a young lady can fully comprehend how hard it is for a young man to ask her. This is not something he does on a whim or for entertainment, indeed not most times! He must want to do it very much to risk being made a fool. Don't say no too quickly. If your reason is that you don't know him or you're worried about what the other girls will say because he's not "cool" enough, think again. While it is true that you don't want to make a mistake, protecting yourself from adventure and the risk of the unknown could mean saying no to something God has for you. You cannot truthfully tell a boy that you've decided to answer no after praying about it if you knew from the beginning that you would say no. Try to lay down preconceived ideas and think objectively. You may think he is not your dream man, but how do you know who your dream man is? He may not even exist. You may know some things about this young man, but *you do not know him*. That's what dating is for: getting to know someone.

If you must say no, be very certain in your own mind and very clear in your response. Don't be confusing or consoling. Just say no. A no should be final, not an uncertain *ask me again in six months, maybe*. If you tell him what's wrong with him, he may be left wondering if you'd date him if he changed something. Just make it a clear, simple no.

You should feel a little privately flattered that he thought you were nice enough to ask; don't think, *what was he thinking; we're not even in the same league!* This is not funny business, no matter who it was. Don't tell everyone how amusing it was that he asked you. In fact, it's best not to tell anyone besides advisors, such as your parents. He may not be for you, but he may be just the man for someone else. You could ruin his chances with other girls by making a fool of him. Damaging his reputation is not worth any fun you could have at his expense.

HOW DO YOU DECIDE?

Unless you know one hundred percent for sure that there are

reasons you could not marry a man who asks to date you, it is only fair to give him a chance. Assume the best about any young man. Be open-minded. Just because he never crossed your mind as a potential husband doesn't mean a thing. Many a happily married woman has confessed that she never imagined falling in love with the man she ended up marrying. He might be shorter than she or younger than she. He might come from a looked-down-on family. He might not fit her idea of "handsome"—or at least not the one she had before she met him. The little twerp from the grade below you in school who always talked too much may turn out to be an admirable young man. The un-cool, too-quiet young man you met at a youth function may be a deeply sensitive and caring man who would make a woman feel special.

Don't protect your life from all chances of adventure by screening men harder than God wants you to. Expand your mindset. Consider the possibility of being won over by someone you didn't like before they liked you. Men used to be permitted to do more wooing than they sometimes are today. Now we tend to have everything so neatly tied up that we feel we have to make a permanent decision about a young man before the first date. This doesn't seem quite fair to him. Besides, being pursued and wooed is an enjoyable part of the courtship process!

One of the ironies of women being too picky is that they feel most young men are not spiritual enough. We ought to be careful with this—who are we to say *we're* so spiritual? If a young woman is spiritual, she should consider it a good sign that a young man has chosen her. Surely he also wants to do right if he is considering marrying a spiritually strong young woman. If he's spiritually lazy and has impure intentions, he would likely look for an easier young woman and not suffer stomach ulcers waiting for your answer. All young men have the potential to become much more than what they are at present. A little encouragement and affirmation could do amazing things for them.

Our current feminist-influenced culture is pretty brutal for men. It can be assumed men are up to no good just for being alive. Men treated in this way might just live up to it. Unfortunately, in our country's gender-confused state, men may be praised for feminine qualities and criticized for masculine qualities. This is confusing as well. It is important for Christian women to accept men for who they are and accept the role God has placed them in. The Bible tells us wives are to respect their husbands: "the wife [must see to it] that she respects *and* delights in her husband [that she notices him and prefers him and treats him with loving concern, treasuring him, honoring him, and holding him dear]" (Ephesians 5:33 AMP). Women who are too critical will find it difficult to live this out.

NOT PERFECT, BUT PERFECT FOR YOU

Don't be afraid to develop a relationship with an honest young man who is growing in his Christian life and welcomes input from others, particularly authority figures. Give him space and a chance just as you'd like him to do for you. The call in our churches today is not only for young men to rise and be strong but for young women to rise and stand beside them.

I would not encourage anyone to date or marry a man they have a bad feeling about or who has known problems or unsavory rumors surrounding him. But if your reason for saying no is that you do not know him or you are struggling with personal fears, don't be afraid to give him a chance.

Young women can get so focused on whether the young men are mature enough for them that they seem to assume they themselves are really something special. Don't forget that you have lots of room to grow too. On average, Christian young people marry relatively young, most of them before science would say the brain has completely matured. Both partners lack the wisdom that only time and experience can bring. Both are quite young in their Christian lives, considering the length of their entire lifetimes. If you marry in your early twenties, both of you are just going to be somewhat immature.

This is okay.

When I think about our wedding now, I feel like my husband and I were such kids. (He was twenty, and I a cool twenty-two.) I can see that he was immature in many ways, but I can see I was immature too. And we both imagined at the time that we were seriously grown up! Getting married and facing life as partners did grow us up—it helped anyway—and it was a wonderful way to do it. If we had waited till we were both fully mature to get married, we still wouldn't be married.

Through the years, we've balanced each other with opposing strengths and rubbed the sharp edges of our weaknesses together, so they've dulled a bit. We're still doing it: still blessing each other, irritating each other by spells, and making each other into better people one way or another.

All this to assure you I did not marry a perfect young man. I might not have married him if I had gone by all the lists. The thing is, I had my own weaknesses and failures—he probably would not have married me if he had gone by the lists. We did not marry as near-perfect Christians but as baby Christians who misunderstood each other, hurt each other's feelings, and were sometimes selfish—and we still are sometimes. But love covers a multitude of sins, and every time we are tempted to zero in on the other's faults, we remember our own, and we know we're both still growing. We're in this together.

Instead of searching for the perfect romantic partner, focus on becoming a good romantic partner yourself. Are you prepared to be an unselfish and loving wife? If God wants you to marry, he can bring the right person your way. Don't underestimate the young men right around you while looking for someone exotic and too-good-to-be-true.

Chapter Fifteen

Romance

The desire for romance is, of course, closely connected with finding the perfect romantic partner. If we find the right one, surely we'll experience endless romance. But what is romance anyway? "A feeling of excitement and mystery associated with love." This definition made me smile. Girls tend to be suckers for romance. We are so emotionally charged, so hard-wired to seek fulfillment in being cherished by a special someone. Bring on the mystery and excitement! But romance is confusing. In many ways, our desire is unrealistic and can even become idolatry. Romance is not the same as true love and commitment.

There can hardly be another period in history when people have sought love so desperately and failed so desperately to find it. (Remember the eight thousand dating sites?) Despite the influence of feminism, the hype about "freedom" from traditional male and female roles, and women's assertiveness, romance is still in high demand. Despite the availability of pornography, prostitution, and one-night stands, people still crave romantic love. And despite all the cultural noise about gender fluidity and same-sex attraction, many people are still interested in heterosexual romance. It's clear evidence of God's plan for people.

DESPERATE FOR ROMANCE

In our world today, people have elevated personal feelings and interests over commitment, rushing blindly from one dating relationship to another. Engagement promises and marriage vows are easily broken. This lack of commitment is caricatured by the alleged account of a young woman riding in a cab to meet a date she had arranged through a dating app. As she rode, she continued scrolling on her phone to see if a better option would come up before she arrived. She was fully prepared to be unsatisfied with her date. And fully unprepared to make the foundational commitments necessary for the love she sought.

People seek romance vicariously through romantic books, movies, songs, and tabloid gossip. They turn blindly away from heartbroken spouses and children in their selfish pursuit of romance. They become entangled in affairs, leaving a trail of broken relationships behind them. Our culture of casual hook-ups, one-night stands, cohabitation, divorce, and remarriage is producing everything but romance.

Oddly enough, while the barometer measuring the actual level of romance in America today continues to fall, cultural expectations of romance are increasingly elevated. Everybody wants what few are finding. Marriage has shifted from being primarily about a partnership to being a pursuit of personal happiness and fulfillment. This pursuit leads to cohabitation rather than commitment, chosen barrenness, and same-sex marriages. This is also what makes being married harder and more complicated than it used to be.

We have more marriage counselors and books than ever, but not many happier marriages. Everyone's expectations are sky high these days. It used to be enough for a man to "bring home the bacon" and bring himself home every night. Now the paycheck may be barely acknowledged; a man is also expected to bring flowers, gifts, and takeout. He should help with the housework when he gets home, play with the children, and get up with them at night at least half the time. Also, he should change diapers. These changes are not all bad; men should be considerate and involved. However, we should be aware that today's wives can expect quite a lot from their men.

We seem to have forgotten what marriage is primarily about. We stuff a pretty big package into a few promises: we want emotional gratification, sexual satisfaction, intellectual fulfillment, and of course, financial stability, plus a few handsome and intelligent children. If we don't get all of these things, we tend to blame our husbands. Our craving for completion in all things makes it hard to get married and scary to choose the right one. If he doesn't fill all these things, did I choose wrong? Or is it that no man can be everything?

I am guilty. I definitely married my husband because I thought he would make me happy. I liked his mind, his humor, and his looks. I thought we could have a good time together in life. We *have* had fun in the past seventeen years, but not nearly enough fun to hold us together without commitment. Together we've survived financial leanness, depression, sickness, exhaustion, babies, temptations, failures, anger, disappointment, and sometimes just plain apathy. We have not been madly in love for every minute of the past seventeen years. But our commitment to each other holds, and because we stick by our commitment, we experience true love and, to a certain extent, romance, but not unrealistic storybook romance.

MARRIAGE IN THE PAST

In times past, love was not the focal point of marriage. Love was something that would hopefully develop between a well-matched couple, but not a prerequisite for marriage as it is in many parts of the world today. A couple was actually viewed more as business partners than soul mates. Marriage was primarily about family connections, daily survival, children, and the economy; that's why marriages were arranged. Matching social statuses was crucial—a peasant must marry a peasant, and royalty had to marry royalty—family compatibility mattered greatly since families tended to live together in patriarchal communities. Matching occupations was also important; bakers married bakers, and farmers married farmers; this made the most sense for success. We have moved so far away from the concept of matching up similarities that, strangely enough, we now insist that opposites attract.[1]

Marrying for love was once a radical, subversive notion. Eloping could get you disowned from your family. Marrying only for love was seen as unstable and dangerous because your love might not last; your passionate feelings could easily change, but all these concrete compatibilities would, ostensibly, hold you together. The trend for love matches is attributed to the 18th and early 19th century revolutions when rights for personal happiness were promoted.[2]

I am not proposing we should give up all expectations for romance; marrying for love is fulfilling. There was some unfaithfulness in these business-contract marriages of the past. It is definitely easier to be married to someone you are fond of and enjoy being with; however, we may have over-corrected. Placing too high a premium on romantic feelings only makes more space for disappointment. It detracts from the actual "business" of marriage: secure family life and, by extension, church and community life. Marrying for love is good, but idolizing and over-emphasizing that love can lead to disappointment, which opens temptations to infidelity. If you crave unrealistic romance, you may be tempted to seek it elsewhere when your marriage falls short of your expectations. Marrying for love is more fulfilling but perhaps more fragile than the practicality of historical arrangements. Many people today consider less than ideal what their grandparents would have seen as normal and functional.[3]

We need a firm focus on the bigger picture of what marriage contributes to the world. Marriages are not primarily places for us to find personal happiness: they are very personalized spaces for us to serve Christ. True love and romance result from our commitment to our spouse; it is not something we can demand. Like happiness, romance is a by-product of something else that is difficult to seek in and for itself. True love grows in commitment and boundaries; in many ways, it comes after, not before, which is the concept behind arranged marriages.

If you marry, I hope you marry for love. I hope your love produces a little mystery and excitement now and then. Just keep in mind that marriage is not all about romance. The courtship period will be high on excitement and mystery as you get to know each other more deeply and focus intently on your relationship. Becoming one in marriage will change the dynamics of your relationship. This is normal. Being together in marriage reduces the level of mystery and excitement that created such intensity before marriage. The high we experience during courtship is unsustainable. We couldn't cope normally with that level of tension for a lifetime! Remember that romance is abnormally portrayed and elevated by a culture hungrily seeking soul satisfaction in the wrong places. You cannot find eternal happiness in a person: only God can meet your soul's deepest needs.

Chapter Sixteen

Breaking Up

I know. You're wincing and fervently hoping you never need this chapter. Breakups are the messy side of romance we don't like to think about. Breakups tend to be awkward and unpleasant. They're natural fodder for gossip: *What happened? Do you know who did it? Why? Well, I always wondered... When they started dating, I said...* and so on.

Everyone hopes to date. No one hopes to break up.

BREAKUPS ARE NOT A BAD THING

The reality of dating is that breaking up is a distinct possibility. It should be a viable option when you say yes, because if the relationship is not working, you need an exit plan. On the whole, we are too afraid of breakups. And we are probably all guilty of being morbidly interested in others' private details. We've created a culture that is perhaps too congratulatory on first dates and that makes couples feel too much like failures if they break up. Our current dating culture suggests you better have prayed enough to be sure of this thing before you even started. So when it doesn't work out, it can seem practically a sin. And we are all far too interested in what part of the formula failed. Fear of breaking up can prevent girls from dating young men they don't know very well. Since she isn't sure if she'd marry him or not, she says no to be on the safe side.

I had never spoken to either of the young men whom I dated before they asked me for a date. I had seen the man I married only a handful of times before we began dating, and I did not even know his name before he asked me. I appreciate that my parents had a fairly relaxed approach with their daughters in dating. Of course, they wanted to be sure we were dating sincere young men, but their mentality was to give a young man a chance if we didn't know of any disqualifications upfront. I think they understood there was no way for us to know how we felt about a young man without spending time with him, also that a man deserves a chance to try to win a woman.

We tend to think of success in terms of favorable outcomes: if someone gets married, their courtship was a success. But success is accomplishing what you set out to do, and in dating, that might mean sometimes figuring out you do not want to marry this person. A dating relationship is not binding; it is an opportunity to get to know someone well enough to see if you'd like to be married to them. If you realize you would not, that's success too. Breakups, though not fun, are not a sin or disgrace. Sometimes they just need to happen. It is like anything else unpleasant which needs to be faced maturely, handled graciously, and moved on from.

So let's throw off the stigma surrounding breakups. Instead

of responding with shock and morbid curiosity, say something like, *Hey, obviously it wasn't working out for them. Glad they figured it out before they got married.* Support friends who have broken up in any way that is helpful and encouraging to them. Unless you are a close friend, this probably just means curbing your curiosity, including them in your social plans, and treating them as usual.

It might help to calm some of the hype around the first date. We have strongly overcorrected on the casual dating scene my grandparents described. In those days, young folks went out with each other randomly until they found someone they wanted to "go steady" with and decided to marry. I was intrigued one evening at supper with my grandparents; my grandma said casually, "I met one of my old boyfriends at the mall today."

"Did you wish you'd married him?" Grandpa said, smiling.

"No," said Grandma, also smiling.

We granddaughters also enjoyed her story of how she'd gone on a blind double date. Unimpressed by her surprise partner, she rode staring out the window, refusing to speak to him.

Casual dating had its disadvantages. But now, by the time a young couple ever makes it to a first date, the young man may have been praying about the girl and talking to trusted people about her for a year or more. He has sweated bullets over the possibility of a no. He may have been thoroughly vetted by the girl's father. He shows up for the first date awkwardly toting an expensive bouquet to declare his feelings for a young woman he barely knows yet.

Typically, they must take a picture on the first date. And they must share the picture because, as some young ladies pointed out, if you don't, people will take unflattering photos of you on the sly and pass them around—and I have seen this to be correct. But sharing the picture and their new relationship status unleashes an instant flood of excited congratulations from everyone they know, thanks to our modern communication capabilities. Some couples cruise confidently toward the marriage altar in the following months. Others aren't so confident. They begin to realize that they'd be happier on the outside of the relationship. But how to extricate oneself gracefully after all the hullaballoo?

A couple should never feel so much pressure that continuing into marriage, in spite of doubts, looks simpler than ending the relationship. One woman described the social pressure she faced in a large church group setting where seven young couples began dating around the same time and did everything together. "There was tremendous peer pressure, and it would have been nearly unthinkable for any of us to break up," she said.

WHEN NOT TO BREAK UP

Before we talk about knowing when to break up, be assured that hitting some speed bumps as your relationship progresses is perfectly normal. The first hint of trouble is not a sign that you shouldn't be together. Even the best marriages are not straightforward. There are always things to work through when two people, no matter how compatible, spend hours, days, and years trying to mesh their lives. Courtship is a time to discover what some of your conflicts will be and how you will deal with them. How you deal with them is almost more important than what they are. Your ability to express yourself and relate well with others is key to a successful marriage.

It is better to face some conflicts and struggles while dating. I've heard it said that some couples fight before the wedding and some fight after, implying that those who face conflict before marriage have an open, realistic relationship and are more prepared for reality. Don't squash doubts, fears, and questions that pop up while dating. Discuss them with your boyfriend and other trusted people where appropriate. Learn how to get things out on the table and work through them together. Burying things never makes them go away; they will keep popping up between you. Usually, one of the partners tends to be the initiator of difficult discussions, but the other can't always wait for that one to lead out. Learn how to be more straightforward if this is hard for you. It will make life easier for you in the long run. The opposite is also true; if you are an aggressive and straightforward person, you may need to tone it down for the sake of a less aggressive partner.

When I was dating my now-husband, I thought semi-seriously about breaking up with him near the beginning of our relationship. The excitement of getting to know each other was quickly used up, and we struggled to break through to the next level of our relationship; the attraction level was low for both of us at that point. Each of us, unknown to the other, wondered if we wanted to continue. Thankfully, the breakthrough came, and feelings came with it. If you experience such doubts, give your relationship enough time. Of course, on the flip side, it should not take an entire year to figure out you don't enjoy being with someone.

Honesty is an essential trait in a man that makes up for other shortcomings. If your boyfriend confesses past or current struggles to you, appreciate the honesty and don't overreact. Voluntary confession—not confession after being discovered—and a desire for accountability are positive signs of spiritual growth. A certain level of struggle is normal. You want him to be honest with you. You should want to be honest with him too.

Depending on the battle, include others in your conversations—you should not be each other's accountability partners at this point in your relationship.

The second time I considered breaking up with the man I married was when he confessed some failure. I did not want to marry someone who would never find victory; however, his openness with both me and his church indicated that he sought victory. I also had failures. Neither of us met the by-the-books requirements for Christian marriage success. (This is why I don't like when girls hold out for a super-spiritual boyfriend.) One of the things that reassured me at this time in our relationship was when his pastor bluntly asked me, in front of my boyfriend, if he'd talked to me about what he'd confessed. Thankfully I could say yes. It gave me security to have adult involvement.

It is not fair to break up with someone simply because he has had a struggle. I say this carefully, but if he confesses it on his own rather being found out, he is open to accountability, and both of you can seek counsel from someone trusted, don't be afraid to move ahead. We are all broken, and we all need a Healer. You need to be afraid of the hidden and found-out-by-accident things, as well as arrogance and secrecy that resists accountability and will not receive input from parents, ministry, and mentors.

A man who wants to continue enjoying his sin will not tell anyone about it. Confessing his struggles indicates that he wants to find freedom. In ascertaining whether a young man is earnest about battling this temptation, look for defensive clues, such as downplaying it as not a big deal or implying that he can overcome it on his own. These show that he is not viewing the problem seriously enough and is unwilling to do battle with it.

In our culture, it is probably more common to have been

exposed to pornographic material on some level than not. The prevalence and availability of pornography and immodesty, in general, can bring fear to women as they wonder how it's possible for their husbands—and someday their sons—to live above sexual temptations. However, sexual sin is not a newly invented evil. There have been other places and times when sexual degradation was common. There have always been those who were faithful. We have the same God to see us through.

Both of you need to understand that marriage will not cure the desire for pornography or any other sexual temptation. Becoming sexually active can increase sexual temptations in some ways. I do not understand or believe the teaching that the quality and quantity of sexual relations at home affect the level of temptations married people experience. We must learn to control our sexual urges before we unleash them inside the boundaries of marriage. Marriage is not a sexual free-for-all; it is an exclusive relationship held by vows within certain limitations.

WHEN TO BREAK UP

I did break up with a young man before I dated my husband. There was nothing wrong with him as a person, and I think he would have been good to me. I just didn't enjoy being with him and felt trapped in the relationship.

Two young ladies who broke up both said that family members pointed out that they weren't happy with the young man they were dating. So be open to the observations and opinions of your family and closest friends. Remember, family involvement can make arranged marriages successful, and even though we don't practice the concept to that extreme, healthy family involvement is integral to the success of your marriage. Your family knows you very well, better than you know yourself sometimes.

If, after giving the relationship time, you don't look forward to being with your boyfriend and aren't comfortable with him, it is better to break up. More obvious reasons for breaking up would be dishonesty on his part, or not respecting your physical boundaries or parental guidelines in the relationship—or if you cannot feel respect for him. Respect for a husband is a choice in many ways, and wives don't always feel it naturally. However, you should feel a basic admiration for the man you marry. If you can't admire him, he doesn't want to be married to you.

Breaking up does not mean you made a mistake in agreeing to date him. You may have had peace about saying yes, but now you realize saying no would release the turmoil you feel. This is okay. You didn't know how you felt about him; now you do. This is what you needed to know.

If you must break it off, be polite but clear. And don't do it the way I did: I wrote a letter. I should have done it face-to-face. It was an awkward, non-closure way to do it. I understood this the next time I was in the same building with him. Do it in person if at all possible.

Breaking up should happen before you get anywhere near to being engaged. When you accept a marriage proposal, you make a promise that should never be broken lightly. Ideally, you will learn to know each other well before you get to that point. An engagement should only be broken for discoveries of things you didn't know, such as infidelity, unrepented immorality, and dishonesty. If your boyfriend has been unfaithful to you, even if only emotionally—such as having a secret girlfriend on the side—run away. Don't let a smooth talker convince you of his innocence if he's clearly in the wrong. Dishonesty is a huge red flag, even if it's only in small things. If he wasn't where he said he was or small parts of his story don't line up, don't trust him. If he needs to lie about something small, certainly there is a much larger deception somewhere. Troubled people can be masters of manipulation, and you are emotionally involved by this time.

Seek advice from others in such a situation. If multiple people think you would be making a mistake by marrying someone, believe them. There are situations where young women went against the advice of multiple counselors when they got married. This is not a wise move. Don't think that because you are so close to him, you understand him better than everyone else. It is more likely that you are so emotionally involved with him that you cannot see the situation objectively.

If you are not yet dating now, you may find yourself facing an unexpected request for a special relationship someday. Don't say no just because you don't know yet whether you could be married to him or not. If you really don't know, give the relationship a chance. Be open to God's direction and the input of others.

You don't have to know whether your relationship will lead to marriage or breakup—God knows. It's okay to take it one step at a time and trust him to direct your heart.

Chapter Seventeen

The Single Woman

Promise me you won't skip this chapter. I know it's more appealing to read about romance—even breaking up, which proves there was some level of romance! Singleness indicates the absence of romance, which appears dull and so *not* mysterious. Then again, you never know. Romance has a mind of its own.

Even if you hope not to end up being a life-long single, please stick with me for at least three reasons. Reason number one: even if you get married, you need to relate with the singles in your life. Reason number two: statistically, a few of you *will* remain single all your lives. Reason number three: you are single right now—if you are in the targeted audience for this book. You might not consider yourself *single* single, as in well past the age that most people marry, but if you are not married, you are single. All of us, married or not, need an appropriate mindset toward singlehood.

THE VALUE OF SINGLEHOOD

Our culture is hyper-focused on romance, indeed so focused that, as Sam Allberry points out in his book *7 Myths about Singleness,* we have lost the meaning and value of friendship. Intimacy has gotten all tangled up with sexual relationships; we don't value the intimacy of close friendships. We tend to see friends as just people we know and hang out with, and think we need romance for a genuine, deep soul connection. We don't know how to have close, deep, and meaningful relationships with each other. We've gotten intimacy so confused and mixed up with sexual relationships that we can be too quick to imagine sexual overtones in a close relationship.

The Bible mentions friendship numerous times and tells stories of deep and close friendships, such as David and Jonathan's friendship. David told Jonathan, "thy love to me was wonderful, passing the love of women" (2 Samuel 1:26). These men were not single and were both heterosexual, judging by their relationships with women. We may have become so uncomfortable with expressions of same-gender love that we are quick to wonder if David and Jonathan were gay. But we know Jesus also had close male friends; one of them was leaning on him at supper. Our culture has confused us about intimacy and sexuality. We may be too afraid of close friendships.

Fear of closeness leads to loneliness. We can sense the extra depth of loneliness fueled by the corruption of romantic and sexual love around us. People are desperate for romance because they are so lonely. Women give their bodies without marriage commitments because they fear rejection and loneliness. Men develop perversions and addictions out of intense cravings for connection. We all need close, healing friendships and to somehow de-emphasize sexual fulfillment.

We all tend to think, subconsciously, that marriage is superior to singlehood. We know the apostle Paul suggested that it might be better to be single, but maybe that was just Paul's idea. Maybe he was a widower, and it was easy for him to say that. Perhaps nobody would marry him, so he had to take that position. I had a lot more respect for Paul's words after I learned that Jewish culture places a high premium on marriage. An unmarried Jewish man over the age of twenty was viewed with suspicion. Paul had been the best of the best Jews. He had to reject the thinking he had grown up with and studied. For him to assert that singleness is just as good as marriage is worth noting.

Of course, God instituted marriage, and we know it's good and necessary for the world to go on. It's also apparent that it doesn't work out for every person in the world to get married. It is normal to desire marriage, but the desire itself does not demand fulfillment. God also placed a desire for children in every woman, and some women cannot conceive. Legitimate, God-given desires don't always get fulfilled.

Singles are not unfortunate leftovers tagging along like spare wheels in case they can be useful somewhere. God has places for singles to fill: places married people sometimes cannot fill, at least not in the same way. Sometimes God's plans for people have space for just one. One may fit into his program where two would not.

Probably we are all guilty of placing too high a premium on marriage. We get too much personal worth from the idea of being chosen by someone. We tend to minimize the benefits of singlehood: *how could it possibly be better to be alone?* We expect too much from romance and marriage. We go on believing we've got it better even after we find out marriage involves far more than a honeymoon and far more than we thought we signed on for. It's not perfect, but married people still tend to be convinced it's better than being alone, evidenced by thoughtless comments such as, "What? Aren't you married yet?" "What are you waiting for?" "So, tell me about your love life." "Where's the boyfriend?" This kind of talk insinuates that celibacy is less-than, which is not a biblical concept. A person committed to celibacy should be admired, not pitied.

I was convicted of this less-than mindset in my own life when I found myself thinking or saying, "I wonder why he/she isn't married. He/she is nice and not even bad-looking." I realized I could say this about many single people I know. I also realized they were making contributions as they were; they did not need a companion to become useful or necessary. Some of my favorite single people are doing things they could not do if they had families. Why would I waste time thinking how nice it would be for them to get married? I have committed to not saying, "She's really nice; I wonder why she isn't married?"

The reality is that even happily married people are not always happy. As the apostle Paul mentions, a lot of stress and baggage come with being married. It is possible to physically be with someone and feel disconnected from them, especially the older and busier you get. I'm sure singles have times of intense loneliness, but married people can feel lonely too. They face a lot of stress as they have families and gain various responsibilities in home and church life. When I think about my life, most of my stresses come *because* I am married. I accept the responsibilities and challenges as part of a package that accompanies the benefits of marriage. In some seasons of life, the challenges may even seem to outweigh the benefits.

I remember reuniting with an old friend who was still single after I'd been married several years. She looked on curiously as I managed my little family, and I listened curiously as she talked about her life as a single. I couldn't help experiencing a twinge of envy. When she stayed up at night, it might be for a late-night shopping trip or a chat with a friend, not a screaming infant's whim. Her body was unmarred by childbearing. She still talked about dreams for her future. Her life remained open to many possibilities, while mine had narrowed into child-rearing and homemaking. I felt a fleeting twinge of envy, and I think she did too, but in the end, we parted, satisfied that there was joy and trouble enough for each of us in our position in life.

WHERE SINGLES FIT INTO THE PROGRAM

Conservative Christians tend to have highly structured homes and churches that don't have neat boxes to place singles in. By default, singles can get indefinitely lumped in with the youth, which is unfair. We don't want to discourage singles from maturing. Marriage is not a rite of passage into adulthood, but we sometimes act as if it is. The twenty-five-year-old who is married may be more naturally included among the older women at church than the thirty-five-year-old woman who is not. This is ridiculous.

Groups tend to divide clearly into lines based on marriage: we have the youth, the young married, families with young children, middle-aged families, and so on. This clear-cut arrangement becomes confusing for those who did not get married when the majority did. Singles are not stuck in permanent youthful limbo;

they are maturing along with everyone else. If they do not seem to be, maybe it's because of how they are treated. Singles can spend extra time with youth as mentors and mature friends, which is good. It is not good for them to spend all their time with seventeen-year-olds, acting like one of them.

Singles should graduate into adult Sunday school classes and be included in the committees and programs of the church. They tend to have enthusiasm and insight that married people may not because their focus is not distracted by family life. Single people can be a huge asset to church life. I find friendship with singles to be refreshing. As a mom, it's enjoyable and reassuring to connect with other moms about the daily grind of mom things, but it's stimulating to talk with singles on myriads of different subjects. Singles remind me that there's a larger world than my family and its immediate needs.

WHAT ABOUT SEXUAL FULFILLMENT?

Probably the biggest deception to believing that marriage is better than singlehood is the belief that sexual fulfillment is a right. More than one person has said or secretly thought that they don't want Jesus to return before they experience sexual intimacy. The lie that sexual experiences are a right or the ultimate in life seems to be an effect of cultural idolatry.

People in our world can barely grasp the concept of lifelong abstinence. We've been so culturally conditioned to the importance of sex that we may secretly question whether it's even possible to live celibate for a lifetime. The subtle and not-so-subtle cultural messages of the importance of sex are everywhere around us. But not in the Bible. A virgin is no less than anyone else. In fact, in this day and age, a contented celibate person is to be admired as someone with a biblical view of life, a proper concept of self-worth, and the self-restraint many lack. In this sex-saturated culture, celibate singlehood is vibrant proof of the sufficiency of the gospel.

"JUST GIVE IT ALL TO GOD!"

Do you wonder if you are still single because of something you're not doing right? Sometimes we hear things like, "Maybe you haven't given up your will yet, so God is holding out on you." Or we might hear a glowing testimony of a young woman who "gave it all to God," and everything worked out beautifully for her—she suddenly found Mr. Right, walked straight to the marriage altar, and lived happily ever after. I suppose I could claim this. I did face a specific moment where I chose to give up my desire for romance and realized the possibility of lifelong singlehood shortly before I met my husband-to-be at the tender age of twenty. This was a good experience for me, but I do not think it was a magic formula that produced a dashing, dark-eyed man. To say this would be to say that every single woman is still single simply because she has not given up her will to God.

"What if you 'give it all to God'... and *he* (the secret crush of your heart) asks another girl?" A vibrant single asked me this with a mischievous grin and at least a small amount of cynicism. A certain percentage of women will simply not get married no matter how much they give up their longings for marriage. Giving up your right to marriage is not a magic bullet; it is an important step for your soul and could mean the beginning of meaningful singlehood for you.

THE CALLING OF SINGLEHOOD

The state of being single is sort of a funny thing that people gradually grow into. Most people don't purpose in their hearts to remain single; it just happens to them as they continue not to get married and eventually reach an age where it becomes unlikely they will marry. There is nothing inferior about them. Single women are completely normal women who, for unknown reasons, remain single past the average age that many women marry, their husbands having all died in infancy, as one single put it.

How does a young-woman-who-realizes-she-is-getting-older relate to this? She could decide she never liked men much anyway, marriage is totally overrated, and look scornfully down her nose at girls who want to get married. She can choose to live hopefully, believing that a man could be waiting for her around every bend in the road, continuing to dream and put in time. These are two extremes; reality probably meanders back and forth between these two. Learning to live with a mind and heart open to God's will at a young age will help you. If you idolize marriage as the only way you can be happy, you will find it a struggle to lay it down. Apostle Paul seems to say that singlehood is a calling (1 Corinthians 7:24). Jesus says the ability to be single is a gift and that some choose to be single for the kingdom of heaven. Rather than feeling overlooked and leftover, wouldn't it be appropriate to conclude that you've been prevented from marrying for a reason? Instead of feeling like you've been left out of God's plan, what if you concluded that God has an important plan for you that does not include marriage?

What if you don't desire marriage? I have met a couple of girls who claim they would be perfectly happy to remain single. I would not necessarily call this abnormal, but neither would I recommend using that feeling to conclude you are intended to stay single. If you wish to remain single and God calls you to singlehood, then good for you. But if a man asks for a special relationship, every woman needs to open herself to God's leading at that juncture, not conclude it is not God's will because she doesn't want to be married. I am not suggesting that you marry a man you don't want to marry, only that you should consider dating if asked and allow for feelings you may not be aware of to germinate and grow.

If you do not desire marriage, ask yourself why. Are you holding grudges against the men in your life? Maybe you do not have a strong father, or there is tension between you and your father. Perhaps a male authority has disappointed or even harmed you. Maybe you feel disillusioned by a lack of spiritual commitment in the young men you associate with. God's plan for men and women and marriage remains the same, regardless of your feelings. And strong godly men do exist, even if you don't know them.

Do you fear the commitment of marriage and homemaking? If it looks big to you, you're onto something. It *is* a huge commitment. If you marry, some morning after your honeymoon, you will wake up and realize that there won't be any meals unless you make them. The laundry will not magically return to the drawers, and the dust will pile up until yours truly wages war on dirt. Adding children to this scene adds more work and responsibility. But this is not something to fear and run from. We can do the work gladly and well and find deep fulfillment in it. Don't be afraid of responsibility. Learn things now that will help you prepare. Even if you never marry, you may still have your own home to keep someday, or you may help others in their homes.

Whether you find yourself in the state of marriage or singlehood, at present or in the future, remember that following God's direction for your life is the most important thing. Either way, you must lay down some of your dreams and desires. You will be most happy now and in the future if you learn to simply accept your status in life. This includes being okay with the uncertainty of not knowing your future. And do not center your self-worth on your perceived marriageability. Your worth to God has nothing to do with being married.

Chapter Eighteen

Surrendered Living

The perceived model young woman in America today has things under control. She seeks personal security by finding completion in herself and her accomplishments: her degree, her career, her finances, her intellect, and her bucket list. This young lady knows what she wants and pursues it. She doesn't need anything. Oh, she probably has religion stored nearby, like the smartphone in her designer purse, handy for emergencies. Romance would be fun, but that's a bonus she pretends not to want too badly. A man in her life is an extra option for additional happiness. She doesn't really want to become dependent on him or give up her own goals to marry him.

You may find yourself attracted to this type of self-sufficient lifestyle. You'd like to take care of yourself and never be caught needy. The problem is that young women tend to find themselves trapped between their efforts to be self-sufficient and in control and the reality that there are a lot of uncontrollable factors in their lives. *I don't even know what I want to do with my life. I don't know if I'll get married or not. Should I get a higher education and a better-paying job? Move out on my own? Pledge my future to foreign missions? Or just wait around?* It would be so nice if God would write the answers in the sky. Besides being unsure about occupation, there is the enormous question of if and who you will marry.

Conservative young women may chafe against the tradition of waiting for young men to take the initiative in relationships. They have no idea whether a young man will ask them tomorrow or never. They're taught not to flirt or make their attractions known. They could spend years secretly admiring a man who will never ask them, and then be asked by someone they never considered. How do they know whether to say yes or wait on their unrequited crush? Of course, a woman has no guarantee her crush would ask her in a million years. For all she knows, he has his eye on another girl.

It may seem unfair that a young man gets to think about asking a girl for weeks, months, even years before he makes a move to ask her, while the girl has mere days to make up her mind. What would you think if I told you this is good for you? That it is a practical example of the trusting surrender in which we ought to live? Women tend toward control and management in their desire to feel secure. We think we'll be safest if we can control a situation and make things happen. Ironically, attempting to control increases our insecurity.

SECURITY VERSUS CONTROL

Women crave security. Knowing what's happening and what to expect makes us feel more secure. Women are notorious for asking *what, where, when,* and *how.* This is not necessarily bad, but it is easy for women to become controlling out of fear and a desire for security. We can become demanding and feel unreasonably angry when left uninformed or surprised.

It has been said that a woman's besetting weakness is her desire to control. Control is our default setting, which we use to feel more secure. But seeking control of others and circumstances by manipulation or demands doesn't bring security; in fact it is a futile effort that only deepens insecurity. It's impossible to control everything and everyone. Eventually, you may feel no one is to be trusted. No one will look out for you but you. Relinquishing control is the key to experiencing true security. To use a slang expression, *God's got this.* We can relax. He knows what and when and where and how.

Living in surrender to God's will for us means attending to matters only within our sphere of responsibility. Don't try to manage your family, your youth group, or your coworkers unless given a specific responsibility to fill. Life goes much more smoothly if we stay inside our sphere of responsibility.

For you, right now, surrender might mean being okay with the boring job while you wait for something more exciting to happen. It might mean simply serving in your home or helping another mother. It might mean waiting longer to see what opportunity opens up for you. It does mean stilling the desires of your heart and patiently waiting for God to direct your future. Don't break down doors trying to control of your life. Let your future come to you. God is in control of the universe; trust him with your details.

SIGNS OF CONTROL

Here are a few controlling behaviors to consider:

- Insisting on knowing all the details about an event. It's okay to ask for information when necessary, but pressing someone for details, especially if you then find fault with them, is a control method.
- Coming unglued emotionally when things don't go the way you planned. Having a plan is good, but life is not always plannable. You need a basic plan with room for flexibility. This is especially true if you marry and have small children someday. Learn to be okay with glitches and surprises. It does not mean the day or the event is ruined.
- Thinking your way is the only way and trying to impose your beliefs and ideas on others, whether how to hem a dress or how the Lord will return. Other people are entitled to their own opinions. Heated arguing and debating is not becoming to a woman. It's okay to have ideas, and it's okay to share them sometimes. But it's a sign of maturity for anyone not to say everything they think.
- Blaming others for everything that goes wrong. You are never in the wrong because you can find a way to shift the blame onto another person or circumstance. This is a form of dishonesty. We all make mistakes and we need to own them, even if they're embarrassing.
- Being a perfectionist. This can seem like a good thing; the problem is that we likely blame others to keep our reputation untarnished. A perfectionist cannot stop with being critical of herself. She is critical of the

whole world. She has impossibly high standards for herself and other people in her life. Realize that you're not perfect either and people have to put up with you. Perfectionism is a form of pride.

- Hating surprises or changes to a plan. The mere fact that you didn't know what to expect makes you upset, even if it's not a bad change. You get angry at people for forgetting to communicate details or thinking the details were unimportant for you to know. Maybe you feel you deserve to have things planned for your benefit. As my mom used to say to us: "You are not the only pebble on the beach." We all need to take a turn being accommodating and flexible.
- Not trusting other people. Because they're going to forget, they're going to do it wrong. They're going to decide not to do it. They're going to take advantage of you. They don't care about your opinions or your feelings. Mistrusting others is a miserable way to live. The more you doubt other people's intentions, the more things you will find—real or imagined—to mistrust. Give others the benefit of the doubt, just as you appreciate from them sometimes.

Such problems will hinder your relationships and your peace. If you see yourself in some of these examples, that's okay; it means you're normal. Acknowledge the areas of weakness in which you need to grow, by the grace of God. An essential part of surrendering is accepting that we're not perfect.

To live a surrendered life, we need a certain amount of trust in other people, especially our family and our church family. Believe in the abilities and good intentions of others. Maybe they will not do something as soon as or in the way you wish. Perhaps they will never do it. That's their problem, not yours. It is mentally freeing to release our expectations for others and accept them, whether or not their performance is what we would wish. Remember: God works with us even though we don't always please him as we should. He extends grace to cover our imperfections. We, in turn, should extend grace to others.

PRACTICAL LIVING

What about all those big questions I raised earlier? Maybe you don't know what to pursue. Perhaps you're happy with what you're doing now, but you wish you knew what to expect in the future. Finding God's will does not mean discovering some magic formula that will make God unlock the key to your future. Being in God's will is a step-by-step process. If you want God to direct your life in significant ways, you must obey him in small areas. You can't take your own course, expecting God to do big things with you.

In making decisions for your future, seek and accept counsel from authority figures and trusted older people in your life. While they may not want to give you a straight yes or no on whether you should take a specific job or opportunity, they can offer opinions and advice from their experience to help you make a good decision. Obey biblical directives. Keep your conscience clear. Honor the church to which you belong. If an opportunity opens that would cause you to compromise in some area, it's not worth the risk.

As for whether or not you will marry, try to lay that down and leave it in God's hands. Marriage does not solve every question. Should you marry, you have no idea whether you will be able to have children or whether they will be healthy. You have no guarantee of your health or your husband's. We don't have anything promised to us except God's faithfulness. God knows what he's doing with you. You can take a sigh of relief and hand over whatever is troubling you right now. It's not yours to worry about. *God's got this.* Nothing will bring greater security to the girl inside than surrendering to God's plan for her life, no matter what it looks like.

Chapter Nineteen

When You're Grown Up

What do you want to be when you grow up? Do you remember how you answered that question as a child? Little girls may proudly say they want to be a mom. Older girls might hesitate, feeling like their options are unfairly limited. They want to think of something more original. Even schoolteacher sounds cooler than *mom*. Anybody can be a mom; it happens by default to most women, right?

Yes and no. Bearing children and mothering those children are not the same thing. Getting married and being a homemaker are not the same thing either. Being a good mother and homemaker is a choice you make, an important choice.

We live in a culture that devalues home life and the capabilities of women's bodies. Feminism—a movement begun to bring equal rights to women—has not brought greater freedom to women; instead, it has lowered the quality of the lives of many women in America today. Many women feel pressured to enjoy the "liberation" of being in the workforce, as well as have children and keep house. Their husbands might not even support them if they wished to stay home because two incomes per family have become standard. For women with families, this makes homemaking a greater burden rather than a lesser one. Some working women may opt out of marrying or having children in favor of their careers. But having children and raising them is God's plan for women; only women can do it. Obviously, the world would soon end if every woman stopped having children. It's not hard to see that having children and raising them to be decent citizens is very important to the planet.

Feminism has devalued women's roles and women's bodies. Liberal agendas brainwash women to believe in abortion—tearing precious life from the place uniquely designed for it to be nurtured. Now that transgenderism is becoming popular, some young women value their bodies so little that they use hormonal treatments and surgeries in a futile attempt to become male. This is very sad. There are young women in America today who are being permitted to make foolish decisions that they regret deeply a few years later. Your body is a woman's body. God made it. It has a unique design and capabilities. You have a body to bear children and keep a home. If God calls you to that, it is the best place for you to be. No career in the world is more important than raising a godly family.

THE SLIPPERY SLOPE OF FEMINISM

In the beginning, feminism created equal rights for women. At one time, women had no legal rights and were basically the property of their husbands. An early political movement known as women's liberation achieved legal and voting rights for women. The next step was women competing with men in the workplace. It is worth noting that women are primarily interested in competing only at the top: women are not fighting to be plumbers or servicemen; they are fighting to get behind desks, in corporations, and into politics. Women want to rule. They do not want to be at home. This desire to do what they are neither asked nor designed to do is rebellion against God. When people rebel against God, things do not go well. The feminist movement has never been satisfied, and has morphed into an ever larger and stranger beast. Many current topics attached to feminism are clearly against the well-being of women.

The stages of feminism have trended downward, straying farther from God's plan for men and women and family life. Women wanted the right to sexual intimacy without marriage. This led to the invention of the birth control pill and the legalization of no-fault divorce. Before we knew what was happening, homosexual marriage was legalized. Now people want to choose whether they are a man or a woman. Not only do women not want to listen to men, but they also don't want to listen to God. Only God can choose whether we are born male or female.

We end up in scary places when we don't listen to God. How can a woman go against her God-given nurturing instinct to promote abortion? How are LGBTQ rights helping womanhood? How can a woman believe she would be better off as a man so much that she is willing to alter her body? These issues are not about equality. Being a mom is an important role that is being carelessly cast aside. Nobody can be a mom but a mom. But many mothers in America today spend very few waking hours with their children.

One day I took my children to a park after school and observed the other mothers and children there. Some of the moms were in working scrubs; they had just picked up their children at daycare and followed them around at the park, trying to connect with them before rushing home to make supper. I especially noticed how these moms had to beg and bribe their children when it was time to leave. The children were not trained to simply go to the car when told. Instead, they had to be coaxed by promises of something special for supper or assurances that they would come back tomorrow. Moms chased their children and tried to hold their hands as they pulled away, talking brightly about going home to see Daddy rather than enforcing obedience.

I don't see how you could train children to obey you when they are with a babysitter most of the day. I cannot help but believe these moms are getting the short end of the stick. They have been liberated only to work extra hard. They must keep up with their job and still do housework at home. They still care for children with less-than-the-best results.

It is not surprising that this societal train wreck has produced a generation of young people who are not doing as well academically. Many are drug-addicted, depressed, suicidal, experimenting sexually, and doing terrible things like shooting up their schools. Living outside God's boundaries produces so much pain and confusion, especially for the innocent involved.

You've probably grown up in a Christian home with parents on their first marriage. You've probably attended a private Christian school or have been homeschooled, which means you are protected from most of the confusing, harmful rhetoric many girls are growing up with. Because we do not realize everything that is "out there," we may be unaware of subtle influences in our lives. Likely you would not consider abortion, even under desperate circumstances. Even if you thought that boys have it better at times, you would not try to become a boy. But you might think having a career is more attractive than being a homemaker.

The influence for girls to be smart and self-sufficient career women reaches us at times. How important is it to you to have an education beyond grade school or to find identity in a career? You may possess admirable marketable skills; maybe you're a talented photographer, designer, or artist. Are you prepared to let these take second place if God calls you to marry and bear children? Because everything a woman could do is second place to raising a family if that's what God calls her to do. We don't always appear to believe this.

We don't need to be needy, clinging vines, devoid of opinions and abilities; we just need to keep our plans open to what God wants for us. Fill your singlehood well, however long it lasts, with an open mind for whatever lies ahead for you.

WHAT DO YOU WANT TO BE WHEN YOU GROW UP?

You may worry that being a mother and a homemaker isn't easy or fun. But nothing is always easy or fun; life is just that way. It's part of growing up, no matter what you do.

Homemaking is a unique role with far-reaching effects. Why should women want to leave something specifically designed for them, something only they can do, to do what men are already doing? If women aren't happy with it, it would have make more sense to try do it better, not worse! Homemaking is not some second-rate, uneducated, under-valued position, certainly not in

God's eyes and not in the opinion of the family who lives in that home.

If God calls you to marriage and motherhood, he calls you to homemaking. There is nothing you could do that would be better or more fulfilling. We need to believe this, no matter who says otherwise. Subtle attitudes against homemaking may include delaying having children for a long time after marriage or not having many children. Remember, the birth control pill was born in feminism for the sexual revolution—relationships outside marriage. Can a person who wants to serve God participate in this rebellion against his boundaries? This is a serious question. Not every girl will become a mother, but most of you will. Look forward to it. Anticipate it. Prepare for it. One of the reasons young mothers may bog down in homemaking and childcare is because they did not prepare well for the task and may have left their single life somewhat reluctantly. It is good to desire marriage, your own home, and children. Don't be ashamed if that's what you want. The Bible says it is good for young women to marry and bear children, if they have that opportunity (1 Timothy 5:14).

Another interesting verse for women in 1 Timothy 2:15 says that women are "saved in childbearing." Bible scholars have imagined this verse to mean some strange things, but one idea that it seems to suggest is that a woman's salvation involves embracing her role as a woman, illustrated by childbearing, a capability unique to women. Homemaking was not an afterthought of God: *Oh, the men will need someone at home to do the dirty work while doing big things in the world.* Of course not. Being a mom and a homemaker is a treasured and valued role in creating a happy home life.

MAKING IT HOME

Being knowledgeable about interior design and making a home are not the same. To be a good homemaker, you do not need to understand the farmhouse, mid-century, bohemian, industrial, or shabby chic decorating styles. Homemaking does involve the home's appearance, but a comfortable, lived-in, appealing-at-the-end-of-the-day look defies an interior design degree. A house can be very stylish but not look like the kind of place you'd like to live in.

Creating a lovely home includes skills like matching secondhand furniture, combining items both of you brought to the marriage, and using loose color themes instead of rigid and restrictive ones. It may mean blending needs like your husband's desk, your sewing machine, and the children's toys and projects in less than ideal spaces. You might not have the luxury of an office, a separate sewing room, or a toy room. You need to be able to make an ordinary home look nice without spending thousands. Working with a budget is another skill you should possess. You need to know how to manage money and control impulse spending.

A lovely home involves more than appearance. Much of homemaking is an intangible ambiance, a fragrance of a husband and wife's love for each other. Happiness in a marriage is sensed by the children and others who enter your home, as opposed to the awkward chill of two people who aren't getting along, even if they don't fight in public. It involves other unseen things, the emotional and mental health of the mother who sets the tone for homelife with her stability and contentment. It includes the skill of managing enough to get everything done while being flexible enough to work around the unexpected.

A woman makes her home lovely by enjoying her work in it

and enjoying her children, on the whole—all moms have their frustrating days and moments. A homemaker needs personal discipline to get up on time and work when she doesn't feel like it—even when she may not be noticed or thanked for it. She needs to be consistent and loving in training children. This is not a leftover unpaid position for an uneducated person; this is serious business! Embrace the challenge and learn things today that will help you later. Anticipate the day you will likely have your own home. Don't dread it as the day you will be cloistered away from the real world and the things you love stuck in endless drudgery.

LIBERTY AT HOME

Homemaking is creative in many ways. You can order your days the way you want, paint your walls the color you like, design curtains of your choice, choose your menus, and plan your week (within reason—there are always unforeseen things to work around). A woman in her home is her own boss; she does not work under someone who tells her what to do all day.

G. K Chesterton, a brilliant English theologian and journalist, wrote an excellent essay called "Woman," in which he puzzles over why a woman would want to be freed from reigning in her domain, the home. In his perspective, the woman has it far better than a man who goes out to work every day and is bound to his job and to pleasing the public. Chesterton "would favor anything that would increase the present enormous authority of women and their creative action in the home." Rather than eating out to relieve the woman bored with cooking, he suggests she ought to "cook more wildly and at her own will... let her invent if she likes, a new dish every day of her life. Let woman be more of a maker, not less."[1]

Being a homemaker is a lovely, weighty privilege. You get the privilege of creating a comfortable space for a family to live, work, and love each other. Embrace the possibility of being a mom and homemaker when you grow up.

Chapter Twenty

Practical Skills

How can you prepare for keeping a home? You are likely in the stage between schoolgirl and marriage. Likely you still live at home. Maybe you have a job, with a little spending cash in your wallet and the freedom to do some things you like to do. This time can easily be wasted because it lacks structured responsibility. You are free to go out for coffee with your girlfriends or go away for the weekend on a whim. You can spend time with other youth, travel, and enjoy yourself.

I caution you against two things at this time in your life: one is becoming too attached to a free and easy lifestyle so that you find it difficult to adjust to the responsibilities of homemaking. The other is neglecting to use your extra time to prepare for some of the duties you will face if you get married. Here is where we're going to get super-practical. Are you ready?

Your mom probably makes homemaking so easy that you don't even realize her skills. You think you'll just wing it the way she does when you get there, but she didn't start with the level of experience she has now. True homemaking takes full-time dedication.

HOMEMAKING EDUCATION

Part of looking forward to the responsibility and privilege of managing a home involves preparing for that role. Don't be so focused on earning money or attaining your career of choice that you miss learning basic homemaking skills like cooking, sewing, gardening, and preserving.

Homemaking skills have become a somewhat old-fashioned thing to admire from a distance.

Everyone thinks it's great that our resourceful and plucky pioneering great-great-grandmothers spun wool, dyed it, and sewed their clothes by hand. We admire their abilities to make butter and cheese, cure hams, preserve by fermentation, and make homemade soap and quilts, but we don't need these talents anymore because of the ready-made items we can conveniently buy. There is nothing wrong with buying things already made, but taking an interest in some of these almost-forgotten skills can make homemaking more exciting and satisfying. I suspect that some of the boredom and apathy women feel in homemaking coincides with too many conveniences and labor-saving devices. You have to feel differently about your home when you've sewn your curtains, sewed the bedspread from scraps of fabric, baked the bread from wheat you ground, or cooked the jam from berries you picked. We can't jump back into that time, but we should consider what we are losing and how it affects us.

This is another area where our culture has changed drastically with the feminist movement. My mother learned to sew and cook in a public school in the 1970s. Home economics was not an obscure elective—all the girls learned these skills. In the 2000s, girls are growing up not knowing how to wash dishes or tell the difference between a tablespoon and a teaspoon.[1]

Public school home economics classes are not entirely extinct—there are still a few options available, though it is now called Family and Consumer Science—but it is an unimportant class that is the first to go when the budget is cut. Girls are no longer viewed as future housewives—everyone expects them to get a college degree and go to work; therefore, they need to be taught marketable skills. The average girl grows up with her mind on a college degree, not homemaking.[2]

You probably didn't attend a public school, and likely your mother has taught you more homemaking skills than the average young woman of society. However, we can be influenced by the idea that homemaking skills are not in vogue and that we should know how to do more hip and marketable things. I do not discount the value of moneymaking skills; if your hobby happens to make a few dollars, great. It is not wrong for women to earn money, even married women, provided they keep their priorities straight. The problem is losing interest in the value of homemaking skills, things that don't make money but which cannot be bought. Soup from a can will never replace a home-cooked soup. When a woman bakes bread, for example, the whole family feels an interest and pleasure that is more than simple nourishment. Do not overwhelm yourself by learning how to do every single thing from scratch; there is no righteousness in it! But I encourage you to take an interest in learning how to do things for yourself, especially if you have someone who can teach you.

Ironically, in our world today, a woman can take one skill, say cooking or interior design, and be noticed and admired for her expertise in that one thing. But the woman who cooks delicious meals on a budget, makes the home look nice without having a degree in interior design, plus keeps it neat while raising happy, healthy children is somehow just a homemaker with minimal talents. The world's view of homemaking has become seriously skewed. Don't let this confuse you!

Take advantage of the opportunity to learn a beyond-the-usual homemaking skill from your mom, grandma, or another older woman. It's okay to take a little pride in having a skill that's becoming a lost art, such as canning, quilting, or butchering. It's true we can buy our food factory canned, our blankets factory sewn, and our meat factory butchered, but you might wish you knew how to do some of these things someday. And there is a lot of satisfaction in doing something for yourself.

When I was a teenager, my mom was determined that I should know how to clean a fowl. I thought it was the nastiest business ever, and I would *never* want to do such a thing for myself. Getting married and leaving home meant I would never have to butcher anything. Guess what? Twenty years later, my husband and I have raised and butchered numerous batches of chickens. I kind of enjoy it, weirdly enough. Putting your own meat in the freezer is incredibly satisfying, and it tastes better than anything you can buy.

Learn to do things you don't like to do. In a home with a mom and several daughters, it's easy for each to specialize in her favorite task. This is a lovely and harmonious way to operate, but someday it will just be you with all the work. So take a turn doing the things you aren't as fond of doing. A little familiarity will probably make them seem easier. You can't just plan on ordering take-out or paying someone to clean or sew for you. Thinking you will pay to get things done assumes that money will flow freely, and it may not, especially in early marriage. What if financial reverses cause you to need to budget carefully all your life? What if God calls you to a mission field where familiar resources and conveniences are limited? Will you be ready to step up to the challenge?

Learn to manage well. Single girls may be able to get away with being careless with time management because they have some cushion, but someday you'll probably find you simply don't have enough time in a day. When that happens, you will learn more efficiency and figure out what is most important. Prepare now by disciplining yourself to get out of bed before the last minute. Teach yourself to put the book down and get to work or to bed on time. Complete the projects you start. Be prompt; don't make others wait on you or pick up the slack where you haven't fulfilled your responsibilities.

Here are some efficient habits that may make your life easier. Many of these were taught to me by my mother.

- Do maintenance clean-up all the time. When you're baking, put each ingredient away as you use it. Gather all the used supplies into the sink and wash them as soon as you've finished mixing. Wipe up any spills. When you've completed your ablutions at the bathroom sink, clean up fallen hairs and wipe water splashes and toothpaste drips. When you wash dishes, wipe the counters, polish the faucet and wipe behind the sink. When you walk through the house or go upstairs, pick up one out-of-place thing that needs to go to the same part of the house and carry it with you. This makes it easier to prepare for guests because you haven't let things fall into utter disrepair.

- Do a thorough job when cleaning the bathroom. Scrub every inch of the toilet, inside and out. Cleaning the outside of the toilet and wiping the floor around it can make a big difference in a house with small children. For the same reason, wash bathroom rugs weekly or don't even use them. Scrub well around sink and bathtub drains where a mold ring can appear. If you clean thoroughly most weeks, you can get away with a quick wipe-up on a hectic week.

- Try to finish one job before starting another. Moms do need to know how to multitask: sometimes they must make breakfast, pack school lunches, nurse a baby, and ensure everyone's shoes are on and hair is combed in the hour before time to leave for school. But constantly living in multi-task mode becomes mentally overwhelming. This increases when you have small children and are tired from being up at night. On cleaning day, it can be easy to get distracted and start on another portion of the task before finishing one thing, but staying focused is generally most efficient.

- It's the little things that count. Enforce the habit of making your bed when you get out of it and keeping your room generally neat. This makes you feel good about yourself and is considerate if you share it with a sister. It takes no more time to put things away promptly and regularly than to spend a chunk of time later sifting through a discouraging mess. Years from now, on a day when your house is a wreck, your children are sick, you're exhausted and wishing you could run away for five minutes, you can walk into your bedroom at bedtime and find a lovely and peaceful oasis because you've learned to keep your own space neat.

- Manage your money well. There's a good chance you don't have much of it right now, but what you do with a little is pretty much what you'll do with more. Live within your means, not by what others are doing. Consider how much you make per week or month and devise a plan to save some. Plan how much you will give. Decide how much you can afford to spend. Budget for extras, or at least keep track of your spending, so you know where every dollar went. It is easier to budget if you track your expenses first and get an idea of where your dollars are going and where you could save a little. Someday you will probably manage household expenses which can be astonishingly large and involve many small stressful decisions.

- Learn how to plan events. Some women are born organizers, others not so much. It's okay if the gifted organizers tend to plan the birthday parties, reunions, and food committees. However, we all need to learn to be hospitable, and even small gatherings require some planning. A little practice is beneficial, even if it's just planning a backyard cookout and deciding how many hot dogs to buy.

- Make lists. This goes along with being organized. Creating visual goals helps you to be motivated and productive. Make a list of things you hope to accomplish this year, this summer, this week, or today. Make lists of things you don't want to forget, birthdays, prayer requests, recommended books, and favorite Bible verses. You can't go wrong making a note of something.

Take time now to make habits and learn skills that will benefit you in the future. Someday you'll be glad you did.

Chapter Twenty-One

Your Life Today

We all gravitate toward me-centered living. It's the most comfortable way to live. Many influences encourage us in our natural inward focus, from self-help books to advertisements that suggest we need to do whatever it takes to be comfortable and happy. As an unmarried young woman, you likely have time, money, and freedom for yourself in a way you may not experience again, space to do what you want with the least hindrance.

I enjoyed many things about my life in my late teens and early twenties. I was old enough to be considered an adult. I had a car and a modest income. I had some independence without many responsibilities. I could still go home and sit down to a supper cooked by Mom and paid for by Dad. I could go out with my friends for the evening without a care in the world. During this brief period, you have opportunities and freedom in a way you may never experience again. In a few short years, you may be a mother wearily wondering what happened to you. You fell for love and romance; now you have a house and babies.

When we think about getting married, we tend not to think much about the "ever after" part. We dwell on the fun of a dating relationship, daydreaming about how he might propose and how we'll decorate our fairy-tale wedding. We might think about the honeymoon, a little about setting up housekeeping, and a bit about the vague children in our future. But our thoughts often cut off there. I don't think anyone gets married daydreaming about living the life of their mothers or other middle-aged women. Somehow, we don't intend to go there. But as life progresses, that is where we may well find ourselves.

It can be challenging to adjust to housekeeping and childcare. You may look back nostalgically at your lost singlehood some days. Every young person needs to understand that the free and easy single lifestyle of the late teen years is not normal life. It is not the epitome of being grown up; it's more like the last vestiges of childhood. When you're nineteen and tasting independence, you may think: *now this is living. This is being grown up.* But it isn't really. It's a pleasant taste of adulthood without the actual responsibility of adulthood.

In the twenty-first century American culture, many young people try to hang onto this stage as long as possible. They live at home longer, seek more education, put off marriage, and delay childbearing, essentially choosing to be grown-up children. This is why the silly term *adulting* exists. The word appears to be used by some millennials when they have to do responsible things like pay bills, clean the house, or even get out of bed and go to work. By using it, a person implies their own immaturity. What is so bad about getting out on your own, working hard, and being responsible? Refusing to grow up on time is like a toddler who is exceptionally late learning to walk. For a while, everyone makes excuses for the delay, but eventually, everyone will go quiet, thinking, *something is wrong*.

So don't idolize this space you are in now. Enjoy your time and freedom, but don't waste it selfishly on stuff and status and having a good time. It is the selfishness we get so attached to that is so hard to give up for teething babies and mortgage payments and husbands we don't always agree with. Live your life now in such a way that taking on responsibility is not a new and terrible idea.

GET OFFLINE

First, you may need to put your phone down. Worry less about keeping up with everyone and everything online and be more involved in the people around you in real life. Online accessibility is a unique pitfall for today's young people, known as Generation Z—those born approximately between 1995 and 2010. You were born into technology; your generation does not remember life before smartphones. The Gen Zrs of society are gamers, music streamers, video consumers, and social media users. They are sometimes referred to as digital-ites.

As Brett McCracken points out in his book *The Wisdom Pyramid: Feeding Your Soul in a Post-Truth World*, the smartphone experience is entirely self-centered. We focus inward when we are on our smartphones, as opposed to relating with other people or even immersing ourselves in a book, which is essentially getting into someone else's head. It is funny how an invention intended to connect people—the telephone—has evolved into something that can hinder communication with the person beside you.

Online experiences can be absorbing and addictive, and we can easily waste time if we're not deliberate about our internet use. It would be a good exercise for you to track your screen time and challenge yourself to lower it. How much screen time do you average daily compared to page-time with your Bible or a good book? If you lowered your screen time by 20% this week, what better thing would you have time for?

We can be quick to pick up our phones for no reason. Maybe we're bored, unhappy, or have a vague sense we may be missing out on something. Sometimes we use our phones as a shield in uncomfortable social situations. Instead of being willing to feel a little awkward and get outside our comfort zone to relate to someone, we can escape by pretending to be busy on our phones. This is not healthy for developing our social skills. We can also lose interest in developing our hobbies and creative talents by being passively occupied on our phones.

Here are a few ideas for breaking down an unhealthy attachment to your phone:

- Put your phone farther away from you than within arm's length, at least some of the time.
- Put it away and leave it away when engaging with other people. It feels rude and can break the flow of conversation when you regularly pull it out with other people. The unintentional message you may send is that anything on your phone will be more exciting and important than engaging with them.

- Don't pick up your phone unless you know what you're going to do with it. Along the same line, don't go online without a purpose, just to see what you can find. That is a good set-up for looking at something you shouldn't or, at the very least, wasting time.
- Have times like evenings with the family when you leave it in another room.
- Have a "home" for your phone somewhere other than your bedroom. No technology in the bedroom is a good policy; that is the place we tend to have the most privacy, a place we often are in when we're feeling depressed and when we're tired. This combination makes us more vulnerable to wasting time mindlessly online and yielding to temptations.

So put your phone down, turn off the tablet, or close the laptop. Look around and notice what's going on in real life. In connecting more deeply with the people around you, look for things you can do for them.

A HEART FOR SERVICE

It's okay to enjoy your freedom and good times with your friends, but look for opportunities to use your time and energy to bless others. The caring and nurturing qualities that make women excellent mothers can be used to bless others in many ways. Be available to help busy moms, especially if you are not needed a lot to help in your own home. Make it your goal to pay attention to children and become a favorite babysitter.

We have somewhat drifted away from the conservative community tradition of young women working as maids for busy mothers. Girls are often eager to get real jobs and make money.

Moms may be reluctant to ask for help because they feel like they can't afford to pay a girl what she can make at a real job. Moms may sometimes think that asking for help is an admission of failure.

Maybe you could make a generous offer to help a busy mom for free or assure her that you don't expect much pay. Offer her a day a week, a few hours a week, or even just one time. Don't show any judgment about the way she does—or does not—keep house. You may think you'd do things differently. However, suppose you were getting up several times a night with a baby, still recovering from that baby's birth, trying to potty-train a stubborn toddler, and still learning how to juggle housework and childcare. In that case, it could look a little different.

I had caesarian births with all my children, and I can tell you that having a maid at your lowest, neediest point is not easy. Here are a few tips for how to be a good maid:

- Respect her ways of doing things, even if your mother taught you something completely different. Maybe your family's way of buttoning the second button instead of the top on dress shirts saves stress to the top button, but you weren't hired as a how-to consultant. Ask her how she likes the towels and socks folded. The whole family will probably be unimpressed if you change things.
- Observe and remember so you can go ahead without asking many questions. When a mom is tired and not feeling well, trying to tell the maid what to do seems like more work than it's worth. Take note of what towels go in which bathroom and what days she does specific tasks. Little things, such as replacing things

exactly where they were after moving them to dust, can feel like a big deal.

- Be sensitive to her personality and mood. She might be dying for some adult conversation and would love it if you'd chat with her. Or she might feel overwhelmed by too much chatter, laughter, or singing, especially if she's tired or unwell. Take your cues from her.
- Incorporate childcare into your work where you can. Little ones love to tag after someone who gives them attention. Let them carry a rag to help scrub or hand you the clothespins. One of my maids told stories and sang songs to my children while she worked, which they adored. Ask if it's okay to read them a few stories.
- Finally, communicate. Don't be too proud to ask if there's anything you should be doing differently. You're in another woman's house doing her work, which might be hard for her to accept.

Of course, there are other opportunities for service around you. Schoolteaching is a service-oriented job ideal for young women and a great way to learn responsibility and develop relationship skills. It may not feel prestigious or pay as much as you'd like, but it's a tremendous opportunity to bless children, their families, and the church. Children's daycare, nursing, and care for the elderly are other opportunities uniquely suited to women's nurturing gifts.

If you have an occupation that is not service-oriented, I recommend using some of your free time to volunteer: help busy moms, assist with church projects or programs for community children—whatever opportunities are available to you. Don't tie yourself so tightly to a career and good times that you never have time for voluntary service opportunities, outreach efforts, or mission trips. If you have a job with a good income, bless others by giving. I once met an eighteen-year-old girl supporting half a dozen Haitian orphans through Christian Aid Ministries. I was suitably impressed.

Another service area would be attention to the elderly in your church or community. Maybe you know an older or disabled lady who would be grateful for someone to pick up her groceries and prescriptions, take her to doctor's appointments, cook for her, or even just visit. Look around your community for opportunities. Don't be shy! Serving involves getting outside our comfort zones sometimes. You will find fulfillment in service to be greater than a night out with friends. Living in a giving way will help to prepare you for the sacrifices of family and church service that may be in your future.

Maybe you won't get married. The same attitude of service applies to people who remain single. If you never have your own family, you can choose to be busy, happy, and fulfilled by blessing those around you with your time and talents.

Paying attention to the needs of those around us makes us happier and helps us develop Christlike character. Scripture tells us that caring for the needs of others is the same as doing things for God: "For I was an hungered, and ye gave me meat: I was thirsty, and ye gave me drink: I was a stranger, and ye took me in: Naked, and ye clothed me: I was sick, and ye visited me... Inasmuch as ye have done it unto the least of these my brethren, ye have done it unto me" (Matthew 25: 35, 36, 40). There are many Bible verses about the importance of loving, giving, and serving others. Finding as many as you can would be a good devotional exercise.

The first epistle of John has the theme of loving God by loving others and would make a great book study for unselfish living. Love for God and love for others go hand in hand. Love for others is evidence of our love for God. A loving, giving, serving girl is beautiful inside and out. She is secure in God's approval and knows the joy of putting others first.

Acknowledgments

I am indebted to various people who contributed to this publication.

My husband, Lyndon, from whose ideology I shamelessly borrow. Thank you for being my greatest supporter and my self-publishing partner.

My mom, Christine Diller, for her input on the manuscript. Thank you for always being encouraging and supportive.

Christine Sensenig, for helpful critique and motivating interest in this project.

Anne Gehman, who offered a valuable perspective and honest criticism.

Rueben and Liz Luthy, and Luke and Lisa Bennetch, for offering insight and clarity from their experience.

Jennifer Perfect, whose editorial expertise performed magic on the manuscript. It was a pleasure to work with you.

Lucrecia Mejia, for being thorough and for asking questions.

The many young women with whom I have had the pleasure of relating, who asked honest questions and sought inner loveliness.

Notes

CHAPTER ONE: "BODY IMAGE"

1. Joan Jacobs Brumberg, *The Body Project: An Intimate History of American Girls* (New York: Random House, 1997).
2. Holly Riordan, "How Much Do Models Weigh?" *The H Hub,* October 11, 2018, https://thehhub.com/2018/10/11/how-much-do-models-weigh/.
3. Megan Garber, "The Weird Athleticism of the Victoria's Secret Model," *The Atlantic,* December 9, 2015, https://www.theatlantic.com/entertainment/archive/2015/12/the-weird-athleticism-of-the-victorias-secret-model/419589/.
4. Alex Bodkin, "What You See Isn't What You Get," October 9, 2017, https://alexlbodkin.com/posts/2017/10/9/photo-retouching.
5. "Yes, Modeling is HARD Work," *My Model Reality,* July 13, 2020, https://www.mymodelreality.com/post/yes-modeling-is-hard-work.

CHAPTER TWO: "THIN CULTURE"

1. Sierra Schrodt, "Eating Disorders in the Modeling Industry" *Medium,* April 29, 2019, https://medium.com/@sierra.schrodt/eating-disorders-in-the-modeling-industry-6327968ad34d.
2. Holly Riordan, "Why Are Models So Skinny?" *The H Hub,* September 12, 2018, https://thehhub.com/2018/09/12/why-are-models-so-skinny/
3. "Warning Signs And Symptoms," *NEDA,* accessed March 2022, https://www.nationaleatingdisorders.org/learn/by-eating-disorder/anorexia/warning-signs-symptoms.

CHAPTER THREE: "MODESTY DEFINED"

1. Crystal Renn, *Hungry: A Young Model's Story of Appetite, Ambition and the Ultimate Embrace of Curves* (New York: Simon & Schuster, 2009).

CHAPTER FOUR: "BECOMING BEHAVIOR"

1. James Strong, *Strong's Expanded Exhaustive Concordance of the Bible* (Nashville: Thomas Nelson, 2009), s.v. "becoming."
2. Strong, *Strong's Expanded,* s.v. "sober."
3. Strong, *Strong's Expanded,* s.v. "discreet."
4. Strong, *Strong's Expanded,* s.v. "chaste."

CHAPTER SEVEN: "HOW DO YOU FEEL?"

1. "The Seven Basic Emotions: Do You Know Them?" *Humintell,* June 24, 2010, https://www.humintell.com/2010/06/the-seven-basic-emotions-do-you-know-them/.

CHAPTER TWELVE: "YOUR HOME"

1. "Church Attendance of Americans." *Statista.* Accessed July 18, 2022. https://www.statista.com/statistics/245491/church-attendance-of-americans/.
2. "Child Hunger and Nutrition." *Children's Defense Fund.* Accessed July 18, 2022. https://www.childrensdefense.org/state-of-americas-children/soac-2021-child-hunger/.
3. *Substance Abuse and Mental Health Services Administration.* August 24, 2017. https://www.samhsa.gov/newsroom/press-announcements/20170824.
4. "Growing Up With Mom and Dad: New Data Confirm the Tide Is Turning." *Institute for Family Studies.* June 18, 2021. https://ifstudies.org/blog/growing-up-with-mom-and-dad-new-data-confirm-the-tide-is-turning.

CHAPTER FIFTEEN: "ROMANCE"

1. "When Did Marriage Become So Hard?" *Hidden Brain: A Conversation About Life's Unseen Patterns,* February 12, 2018. https://www.npr.org/transcripts/584531641.
2. "The History of Romance," *National Women's History Museum,* February 13, 2017. https://www.womenshistory.org/articles/history-romance.
3. Eli Finkel, "The History of Marriage: Why Marrying for Love is a Newer Idea Than the Printing Press," *Thrive,* September 26, 2017. https://thriveglobal.com/stories/the-history-of-marriage-why-marrying-for-love-is-a-newer-idea-than-the-printing-press/

CHAPTER NINETEEN: "WHAT DO YOU WANT TO BE WHEN YOU GROW UP?"

1. G. K. Chesterton, "Woman," reprinted from *All Things Considered,* London: Methuen & Co., 1908, *Notable Quotes,* accessed March 2022. http://www.notable-quotes.com/w/woman_chesterton.html

CHAPTER TWENTY: "PRACTICAL LIFE SKILLS"

1. Tove Danovich, "Despite A Revamped Focus On Real-Life Skills, 'Home-Ec' Classes Fade Away," *The Salt: What's On Your Plate,* June 14, 2018. https://www.npr.org/sections/thesalt/2018/06/14/618329461/despite-a-revamped-focus-on-real-life-skills-home-ec-classes-fade-away
2. Cortney Moor, "Why is home economics not taught in schools anymore?" *Fox Business*, June 16, 2020. https://www.foxbusiness.com/lifestyle/home-economics-not-taught-schools.

Selected Bibliography

These are some resources I found helpful in writing this book. Including them in this bibliography does not mean I fully endorse everything in them.

Allberry, Sam. *7 Myths about Singleness*. Wheaton: Crossway, 2019.

Anderson, Ryan. *When Harry Became Sally: Responding to the Transgender Movement*. New York: Encounter Books, 2019.

Brumberg, Joan Jacobs. *The Body Project: An Intimate History of American Girls*. New York: Vintage Books, 1998.

Couchman, Judith. *The Woman Behind the Mirror: Finding Inward Satisfaction With Your Outward Appearance*. Nashville: B & H Publishing Group, 1997.

Ethridge, Shannon. *The Fantasy Fallacy: Exposing the Deeper Meaning Behind Sexual Thoughts*. Nashville: Thomas Nelson, 2012.

Gilson, Rachel. *Born Again this Way: Coming out, Coming to Faith, and What Comes Next*. Epsom, Surrey, England: The Good Book Company, 2020.

McCracken, Brett. *The Wisdom Pyramid: Feeding your Soul in a Post-Truth World*. Wheaton: Crossway, 2021.

Pearcey, Nancy. *Love Thy Body: Answering Hard Questions about Life and Sexuality.* Grand Rapids: Baker Books, 2019.

Perry, Jackie Hill. *Gay Girl, Good God: The Story of Who I Was, and Who God Has Always Been.* Nashville: B & H Publishing Group, 2018.

Rainer, Thom. *I Am a Church Member: Discovering the Attitude that Makes the Difference.* Nashville: B & H Publishing Group, 2013.

Shrier, Abigail. *Irreversible Damage: The Transgender Craze Seducing Our Daughters.* Washington D. C.: Regnery Publishing, 2021

Turkle, Sherry. *Reclaiming Conversation: The Power of Talk in a Digital Age.* Westminster, London: Penguin, 2015.

Webb, Jonice. *Running on Empty No More: Transform Your Relationships With Your Partner, Your Parents, and Your Children.* New York: Morgan James Publishing, 2017.

Webb, Jonice. *Running on Empty: Overcome Your Childhood Emotional Neglect.* New York: Morgan James Publishing, 2012.

Welcher, Rachel. *Talking Back to Purity Culture: Rediscovering Faithful Christian Sexuality.* Westmont: InterVarsity Press Books, 2020.

About the Author

Mary Burkholder lives in southern Mississippi with her husband, Lyndon, and five children ages six to fifteen. They attend Darbun Mennonite Church, where her husband is a pastor. Mary enjoys her family, quiet moments, gardening, walking, reading and reviewing books. People and words fascinate her, which is why she's been writing for twenty-five years. Find all her books at maryburkholder.com.